Praise for *My*

Without the advantage of sight, and perhaps benefitting from a focus that seeing writers fail to achieve, Amy Krout-Horn is able to set to paper the brief twenty-two years of her visual memory (and the years to follow) with unforgettable clarity and passion. Like fellow mixed-blood genius Langston Hughes, Amy Krout-Horn plumbs the depths of the sorrows of her preferred ethnicity and weaves from those tragic threads a tapestry, or Lakota star blanket, of shimmering beauty and hard-won hope. As Hughes did for black writers, and Plath did for feminists, Amy Krout-Horn raises the literary standard for Native American authors everywhere, in both senses of the word, with the publication of this book. Her titanic struggle against diabetes, racial prejudice and her own inner fears and fragilities—described here without mercy—will hit the target with Native American readers, but also with all those who have suffered the slings and arrows of outrageous fortune and come out undefeated. *My Father's Blood*, a masterfully-told story about the blessings and bleedings that can be derived from a Native American inheritance, is actually everyone's story. Regardless of our race, we all must face disease, rejection and even our own mortality sooner or later; it's what we do with it that makes us what we truly are and what we can be. As Amy so aptly writes, "The tenacity and fortitude of warriors were my legacy. The spark of primal power was my legacy. Blindness could steal the sun. It could rob the moon and stars from the night. But it couldn't take the spark, the spark that contained my spirit."

-**Evan T. Pritchard**, author *No Word for Time, the Way of the Algonquin People*, Adjunct Professor, Pace University

"*My Father's Blood* brings the light of understanding to the darkness that can surround diabetes. Krout-Horn's story, told with rich, compelling language and relatablility, shows the fear, the faith and the fortitude which come from living with diabetes. She details, in her journey from childhood to adulthood, the disease's impact on family, friends as well as the journey diabetics travel. Mixing her experiences with the profound impact and influence of her culture, Krout-Horn conveys hope and healing as she puts purpose to diabetes to educate others.

This is a must-read for anyone impacted by diabetes and those wanting to learn more about the disease and its affects. "

-**Jolene Loetscher,** JDRF South Dakota, Media Chair

"*My Father's Blood* is a finely crafted tale of the stresses and successes of living with physical and cultural inheritance. Each chapter in Amy Krout-Horn's journey is written with vivid word textures of visual and auditory imagery. If you are looking for a read to fine the Human potential to balance the physical and metaphysical challenges in life, this story of Last Word Woman, is the last word."
-**Robert Leslie Newman**, President, National Federation of the Blind Writers' Division

"To read *My Father's Blood* is to journey to a land of rare poetic verse, raw images, and beautiful recollections. Krout Horn gives us her story, her heart, her pain, her triumph in a world few have had the opportunity to visit until now. The edginess of her candidness blends brilliantly with the sincerity of her love for family. As you take this rendering journey through the deep clots of blood relations, stay strong and pay attention. You might see yourself reflected in the blistering, healing redness along the way."
-**MariJo Moore**, Cherokee Author of *The Diamond Doorknob, When the Dead Dream* and *A Book of Spiritual Wisdom – For All Days.*

"*My Father's Blood* is an immersive autobiographical novel. The intimate narration herein interweaves one woman's struggle for identity and search for wholeness in the face of illness and loss. Amy Krout-Horn paints for her readers a world that is precise and vivid, and the portrait she paints expresses the remarkable beauty that can be extracted from painful experiences, if only we endure. "
–**Jen Knox**, author of *Musical Chairs* and *To Begin Again*

"Highly honored Native American writer, Amy Krout-Horn is an extraordinary soul-speaker, one so gifted in descriptive brilliance that those so fortunate to read her autobiography, "My Father's Blood," will never be the same.

As Krout-Horn pulls us into her very personal and deeply moving stories, we become one with her. We feel the crush of our own broken heart as she weeps in deepest agonies. We feel the brilliant beams of sunlight pressing our souls as she reaches out and finds the courage to carry on. As she dives into her own soul memories, with crystal clarity and amazing imagery, she teaches us profoundly. We learn, in most intimate and daring ways, how deeply diabetes hurts and how strong a warrior one must become to endure the battle. Compassion is born through us, reverence for life is remembered. This gift to us is only surpassed by the sweet blessings we receive when she finds herself, as she finds a True Being, a Pure and Powerful One, who merges his own greatness with hers and becomes her sweetest lover, her closest friend, her dearest soul-mate. From their union, we all are pulled into the sacred heart of divinity, as One Being, One Heart, One Love."

-**Susan Stephan,** Psy.D., Clairaudient, Author of *Saving Our Children, An Endangered Species*

My Father's Blood

Amy Krout-Horn

ALL THINGS
THAT MATTER
PRESS

My Father's Blood

Copyright © 2011 by Amy Krout-Horn

ISBN: 978-0-9846392-9-8

Library of Congress Control Number: 2011934092

Cover art by Carises Horn

Published in 2011 by All Things That Matter Press

For my mother Cynthia,
whose beauty and nurturing spirit
is equal only to Earth herself,
and in sacred memory of my father,
Merle.

PART I

WINTER SOLSTICE

Song of Failure
(Lakota)

A wolf
I considered myself,
But the owls are hooting
And the night
I fear.

1974

"Don't be afraid of the dark," my father had often said with that paternal tone of certainty that made a five year old feel more secure. "There's no such thing as monsters."

When I peered from my mother's arms over her shoulder into the night's impenetrable new moon blackness, I no longer believed him. The air's frigid bite stung my eyes and I blinked, fighting off the illusion of blindness it cast. Perhaps, according to my father's claims, evil entities did not lurk in the depths of my closet or in the dank corners of the fruit cellar, but here, along the deserted country road, the darkness itself was the monster. Pressing down around us, it erased everything, leaving only a stifling black void. Impaired by thick mittens, my little fingers fumbled to clutch my mother's neck tighter; my rapid breaths clung as frost crystals to my scarf's knitted yarn. I spoke in a whisper so faint it resembled thought more than voice.

"Mommy, I can't see."

Less afraid of the lightless space behind my lids than the night surrounding us, I shut my eyes and heard the dry snow crunch under her heavy boots as she turned in her tracks.

"Look," she urged. "In the sky, above the trees!"

From behind the coils of wool scarf, I lifted my chin and peeked timidly through half-open slits. Grazing the tree tops of a distant pine grove, the horizon danced with a curtain of undulating light. Waves of color, red, gold, blue and green, pulsated, expanding outwards across the December sky. Like a vibrant patch of some future day impatiently anticipating its arrival, light currents flowed, nudging the edges of the present night. The mirage grew larger above the frozen landscape until its grandeur captivated me, and I no longer sensed the oppressive darkness at our backs. Wide-eyed with wonder, I felt her breath, warm against my cheek.

"Aurora Borealis," she said.

The words were so magical; they danced in my ears like song and, for a moment, the sea of liquid light swelled, as if drawn closer to the sound of my mother's voice uttering its name. From beneath the celestial intersection, we watched as the luminosity flowed south, penetrating further into the darkness.

In the time of the Ghost Dance, Lakota warriors had once transformed the great lights into symbol, adorning their shirts with the fiery waves; on this night, nearly a century later, my memory became the collective surface on which the aurora's powerful beauty was being painted. As quickly as the waves had moved forward, they receded, diminishing until, at last, the light existed only as a thin red thread across the northern sky. Tempests of dry white snow leaped from the tops of drifts and danced circles around my mother in the deepening dimness as she walked home, still holding me in her arms.

In the years that followed, a monster, the one that even my father feared would find his only child, came for me. As it unleashed the darkest darkness, I found myself calling on strong medicine hidden in my soul, wrapped in memory like a native winter count. I called on the medicine of Aurora Borealis.

CHAPTER ONE

SUMMER OF THE OLD WOMAN'S TOUCH

The three visitors first arrived during the long dog days of 1975 when the earth baked hard and dry beneath the relentless sun and the night brought no relief from the heat. Like sentinels, they stood in the sultry darkness above the narrow bed, wordlessly watching.

I stared at each of them with a child's wide-eyed fascination: the man, perhaps in his thirties, wore his long black hair in braids that framed the sharp angles of his face; the young round-faced boy, his inquisitive eyes peering above cheeks still chubby with baby fat; and the old woman, her copper skin and her dark hair both lined with signs of agedness. Their moccasins, tanned leggings, and the soft deerskin dress of the old woman alluded to the past and I wondered if we were meeting through our dreams.

But they appeared so tangible; I could smell the faint sweet smoky scent of their clothing and I could feel the damp sheets clinging to my body as the humid night air lay oppressively against my chest. My senses told me that I was not dreaming, yet, trying to lift my head from the pillow to better glimpse the hazy images, I knew that I could not possibly be awake, either. Afraid of this eerie new dimension and the mysterious ones with whom I shared it, I struggled to drag myself into full consciousness.

Tenderly, the old woman bent and brushed her hand across my cheek and I grew calm at the odd and unexpected familiarity of her touch. It was not like the caress of fingertips against the flesh of my face, but rather a cool breath of wind that soothed my flushed skin. As she withdrew her hand, her eyes glimmered with the type of love and kindness I had so often seen in the expressions of my grandmothers. The young boy clutched the fringes of a belt hanging from her slender waist and she lowered her gaze to the small face looking up at her. The man moved closer to the old woman and gripped the boy's shoulder. Their simple yet deliberate gestures spoke of the connection between a father, a son, and a grandmother: they were family.

Who are you? I thought.

The woman's mouth curled at the corners as if she might speak, but she only looked on in silence, the little smile dancing on her lips and promising the revelation of an untold secret. I would not know the visitors' identities or the reason for their enigmatic appearance until years later, but as the low roll of thunder echoed in the west and the leaves of the cotton wood rustled in anticipation of the coming storm, I saw the recognition in each of their faces. They knew me.

The irresistible tug of sleep beckoned once more. The unfamiliar reality from which I had only seconds before tried to escape could not hold me though I now longed to stay. I wanted to learn the meaning that lay behind the old woman's smile. I wanted to understand the knowledge I saw in the man's eyes. Who were they? Why had they come? A jagged finger of lightening veined the sky, illuminating the small room and casting their shadows across my body like a dark weightless shield against the approaching storm. Huge drops of rain fell, drenching the parched earth, their rhythm lulling me deeper into sleep and farther from the ones who knew me in a way that I did not yet know myself.

When I awoke, the August humidity had lifted. The morning air, cooled by the rain, moved through the screen and whispered to me of the changes autumn would soon bring. The maple trees' leaves would transform from the lush green of summer to the brief reds and gold of fall. The dawn would no longer be filled with the robin's song, his migration taking him to warmer climates for the winter. The earth and sky were completing one cycle and preparing for another to begin. I was changing, too. But unlike the seasons and cycles, my changes would be unexpected. Many would be uninvited. Some would be unwelcome. All would change the way I looked at the world and forever alter the way the world looked at me.

CHAPTER TWO

AUTUMN OF BLOOD AND RAISINS

Three pairs of pants. Three pairs of feet. Three pairs of shoes. The view from under the Osceola County Hospital bed did not allow for much more. The small bare foot with the cherry red nails dangled a tan leather exercise sandal from the toes and slapped the wooden sole against its callused bottom with nervous rapidity as my mother crossed and uncrossed her legs. The faded denim bell bottoms rustled around her ankles with each new anxious motion. In the doorway, a pair of scuffed brown loafers sprouted from orange, gold, and green double knit plaid pant legs and tapped their impatient staccato beat against the white tile floor.

"Jane, I need your help here. She won't cooperate and I'm pressed for time. I have a staff meeting in thirty minutes," the voice from atop the unattractive double knit said.

Two institutional white lace-ups with pudgy feet resembling popcorn in the process of freeing itself from its kernel moved closer to the bed. I drew my legs and arms towards my body and retreated to the other side of my cramped fortress, frightened that the adults had decided to resort to more drastic measures and I would be dragged from the only place I felt safe at this moment. The nurse knelt, lifting the blue cotton blanket and letting the harsh fluorescent light creep in. She peered through the bars of the bed rails and I turned my back on her intrusive eyes. None of them had seen me cry and I wanted to keep it that way. They entered my room every couple of hours with a tray of multi-colored vile, syringes, needles, and lancets. They stabbed the tips of my fingers. They drew what seemed like gallons of blood from whichever of my thin limbs was willing to relinquish some. They injected insulin into my legs, my arms, my abdomen, and my buttocks. They inserted needles into my wrist and groin for something called an arterial blood gas. They removed the IV from the collapsed vein of my right hand and pierced the left one. I clenched my teeth. I curled my toes. I balled my fists. But I never cried.

"You are a brave little girl. How old are you?" they would say, slapping another Snoopy adhesive strip on my bruised forearm as if the cartoon character's grinning face was adequate compensation.

"Six," I would say in a whisper, swallowing the pain, refusing to allow it to show itself as tears and feeling sorry for Snoopy that his friendly face had been chosen to cover kids' wounds.

It was a lesson I had been subconsciously learning from birth; my father the teacher, my mother his assistant, I their observant pupil. For six years, I had watched my father's morning regimen from the wooden chair at the kitchen table. As I silently ate cereal, he rolled his bottles of insulin between the rough palms of his hands, the glass clicking against his silver wedding band in rhythm with the faint tick of the wall clock above us. Lifting the syringe to the light over the sink, he would draw the clear liquid into the needle, counting units under his breath as they flowed into the plastic barrel. My eyes never left the sight of his procedure: the swabbing of his scar tissue-bulged abdomen with rubbing alcohol, the steadiness of his hand postured as if he were holding a dart, the disappearance of the needle into his flesh, the unflinching expression that made it seem as casual as brushing your teeth or buttering your toast. He never cried, never complained, even when blood would trickle from the injection site. He regarded it with indifference, absently dabbing it away. More consideration was given to the grape jelly I had spilled on the counter top or the blanket lint that he plucked from my long tangled hair.

Once, after my father had left for the Chevrolet dealership, I found a discarded swab that had gone unnoticed crammed between the bread box and the black tea tin. Retrieving it, I pulled the cabinet door open with the intention of tossing it in the trash, but I stopped when I saw the reddish-brown stain. It must have been lying for several days, for it was dry and no longer smelled of alcohol. Only my father's blood remained upon its soft surface. Without knowing why, I slammed the door shut and stuffed the object into the pocket of my jumper. Later the strange keepsake would be placed in the bottom of my jewelry box and, removing it from time to time, I would perform a kind of secret ceremony. Alone in my room, I would place the swab on my bed and, kneeling on the thin carpeting with my chest pressed against the edge of the mattress, I would contemplate the meaning of the blood stain and the questions it raised for me about my father's condition.

"Doesn't that hurt, Daddy?" I asked one morning again watching my father inject insulin into his bicep.

Time spent with the secret object the evening before had not been fruitful and I decided that I must gather my courage and pose the questions that, for unknown reasons, I had been afraid to ask.

"Sometimes," he said, as he pulled the needle from his skin and tossed it onto the bleached white wash cloth that he used to wrap his syringes and alcohol swabs.

"When it does hurt, don't you want to cry?"

An uncomfortable silence followed, causing me to regret my childish curiosity, until my mother cleared her throat, turning from the sink, her hands soapy from the breakfast dishes.

"Your Daddy is very brave and he wouldn't want to cry because it might make you and I feel sad."

Her simple, yet logical explanation for my father's stoicism resurfaced as I buried my face into the crook of my arm and let the tears run to my chin. They pooled on the cool hospital linoleum beneath my cheek. Nurse Jane's gentle coaxing broke into my thoughts.

"Amy, I promise if you come out there won't be any shots or finger pokes. The nutritionist wants to talk to you and your mommy about a special new diet."

Ignoring Jane's request, I dug my hand into the pocket of the seersucker hospital robe and withdrew Stuart. His shiny black bead eyes peered at me through the gray fur of his tiny face and I brought his soft pink felt ears to my lips.

"I don't think we should come out. Do you?"

Stuart's reply did not come in the form of sound, but sensation. As my fingertips stroked the pink yarn tail and matted fur of his rump, it was clear to me.

"We're not coming out," I said, my back still turned towards the nurse's squatting figure.

The bed squeaked faintly as Jane supported herself against the side rail and heaved to her feet, announcing that Stuart and I would remain under the bed. The nutritionist exhaled with obvious disgust as the nurse invited her and my mother to join her in the hallway. I turned my face in time to see the tan exercise sandals, the white lace ups, and the ugly brown loafers exit single file through the doorway.

Again, my fingers traced the crusty patch of fur on the mouse's body and memories of how he had gradually obtained the scar pulled at the corners of my mind.

"What is your stuffed friend's name?" the doctor had asked, his kind eyes passing from my sullen face to the small gray lump that lay beside me on the emergency room examination table.

Through a small window, the sun, a fiery red ball, crested the distant rows of dry Iowa field corn that trembled in the autumn breeze, and held my gaze. His voice had not penetrated my cloudy concentration, as I stared, contemplating the world that lay beyond the glass. Across the patchwork quilt of fertile rolling farmland that had once been a prairie sea, on the opposite border of Osceola County stood the rural elementary school where, on any other day, I would now be with my kindergarten classmates. Today was Monday, which meant a new letter person would be arriving. I wondered if the colorful inflatable character would have a vowel or a consonant emblazoned upon its chest. Today was also when a boy's mother was bringing their litter of puppies for show and tell, and we would be having graham crackers with vanilla frosting for snack time. Realizing that I would be missing out on the new alphabet character, the puppies, and my favorite treat all on the same day made my brow furrow with worry and disappointment.

"Stuart Little."

My mother's voice pulled me back into the moment as my silence exceeded etiquette's boundaries and she had grown embarrassed at my unusually rude behavior. The young doctor, unhindered by my obvious attempts to ignore him, had smiled and asked if I had read the book. I rolled my eyes. Of course I had read it. Where did he think I got the name? My mother's patience with my belligerent attitude was wearing thin and she had looked apologetically at the doctor. Dropping my eyes in shame from his understanding face, I busied myself by wrapping and unwrapping Stuart's yarn tail around a finger.

The anger, bitterness, and rage bubbled like acid just below my surface and as much as I tried to keep it from boiling over and burning those around me, I could not control it. It was as if an evil, spiteful little monster had invaded my body and transformed the shy well-mannered child that I had been only a week earlier into someone that no one, including myself, could understand or tolerate. The vicious creature churned my stomach and caused me to vomit. It drove me to drink glass after glass of water at the bathroom sink in the middle of the night, leaving me bloated and still thirsty. But worst of all, it put venomous words into my mouth, which I spat out at the people who loved me.

"I hate you! I'm never coming back here again," I had shouted at my stunned grandmother, as, two days earlier, I stood in her kitchen, clenching my fists.

"I don't think you mean that," she had said, trying to take me in her arms as I wiggled free, buried my face in my mother's waist, and sobbed.

Remembering the scene at my grandmother's house, I had hoped that the doctor's feelings weren't hurt and that he would help me rid my body of the foul unwelcome visitor.

The lab technician arrived with a folder full of papers. The doctor pivoted on his stool towards the desk and examined the results. I watched my parents and tried to translate what their expressions and actions said about the situation. My mother sat perched on the edge of the folding chair as if she would take flight at any moment, her eyes darting from my father to the doctor's stooped head, to me and back again, in awful anticipation. My father had stood beside her, motionless, hands clasped in front of him like a man awaiting a sentence for a crime he did not commit. When his interpretation of my lab report was finished, the doctor had addressed them, using words like "elevated levels of glucose in the blood stream" and "diabetic keto-acidosis". My mother had reached a shaky hand to clutch my father's arm, her bottom lip quivering as tears welled in her exhausted eyes. He had cupped her shoulder and looked past the sterile metallic room to the east where the sun continued its ascent, but not before I saw the single tear that had trailed along his smooth handsome face. The grief that my parents had denied themselves over the years had been released, triggered by my illness. The crux of their lesson seemed as clear as the September sky that held my father's gaze: crying was a precious commodity reserved for, in their times of need, the ones we love.

"Do I have diabetes like my dad?" I had asked the doctor, the tone of the question sounding too mature for the little girl from which it had come.

"Yes," he said.

"Will I have to take shots like he does?"

"Yes."

The doctor, unable to meet my eyes and unprepared to answer such direct questions to a child, occupied himself with the adjustment of the stethoscope around his neck.

"Okay," I said resolutely and held the stuffed mouse in the palms of my hands, offering it to him.

"I think Stuart has diabetes, too. You should check him."

Relieved by my return to what appeared to be a more child-like mentality, the compassionate physician had exhaled and taken Stuart from me. He placed the stethoscope to the small furry body and had declared that I was right. Stuart did have diabetes.

"No," I had said, shaking my head, "You need to take blood from him like you did from me."

He had hesitated briefly, unsure of how far he should allow my imagination to take him, before smiling and asking the lab technician to draw the mouse's blood sample. Swabbing the gray furry rump with an alcohol prep, the tech had inserted a hypodermic needle and drew the invisible fluid from my friend into the barrel as I watched with great concern. To no one's surprise, the tech had left the examination room and returned minutes later to report that Stuart, like my father and I, had juvenile diabetes.

Now, as I lay beneath the bed, I caressed the ragged patch of fur again and again and cried for Stuart's hurt, numb to my own tender flesh. When my mother returned with the dietician, they discussed inappropriate foods and I cried for the birthday parties the mouse would celebrate without cake and candy. The dietician spoke of healthy snacks and I cried for Stuart's dislike of celery and his loathing of raisins. My mother's inquiry about meals on my return to school brought another wave of sobs from my chest as I realized Stuart Little would be the only mouse in kindergarten with a chronic illness. I cried for the alienation, the isolation, and the shame that I somehow knew awaited him beyond the hospital walls. I cried until a merciful sleep wrapped around me and I lay fetal, Stuart pressed to me, my dreams filled with the image of raisins piled in shriveled heaps on an immense table, their color like a dry blood stain against the white cloth beneath them.

CHAPTER THREE

WINTER OF THE DANCING RABBITS

"Do you remember Clarence Howe?"

My grandfather paused, his hand gripping the neck of the guitar that lay in his lap. Looking up from the instrument, he considered my grandmother's question as he watched the blizzard taking shape outside the frosty kitchen window. He nodded, lifted the replacement A string from the table and rested it against the frets.

"I believe that was the winter of ..."

"48. It was either January or February of 1948," my grandmother said, completing his thought.

"Tragic. A storm just like this," my grandfather said, shaking his head.

I stood at the gas stove, on a low wooden stepstool that Grandpa had built for such occasions, and stirred the hamburger and onions with a wooden spoon, growing more and more curious about the identity of Clarence Howe. Out of respect, I didn't interrupt their enigmatic conversation, though. The aroma of the frying meat made my stomach grumble and I turned the heat up under the cast iron pan, wiping my fingers on the over-sized apron that Grandma had wound several times around my slim waist. They continued the part verbal, part telepathic dialogue that belongs to those who have shared many years together.

"His wife was—," she said.

"The youngest of the Forester girls. Wasn't she—"

"A librarian. I always thought—" she replied.

"Yes, so did I," he agreed.

Only a faint glow of daylight remained above the neighboring rooftop as I watched the wind carrying snow from the empty field across the gravel road and sculpting it into an impassable drift in front of my grandparent's house. No one would be traveling down this road until the plow passed through in the morning. The thought of being cut off from the rest of the world soothed me. I felt safe. I felt understood. I felt wanted. It didn't matter whether or not I was included in their conversation. At least Grandpa and Grandma weren't afraid to have me sleep over. Not like my first grade classmate who had come to school a week earlier with nine pretty pink envelopes containing invitations to a birthday sleep over party. Nine happy seven-year-old girls went home with the carefully hand-printed cards, crafted by the mother who would be their hostess, in their book bags. I returned from school, my bag empty but my head full of disappointment and confusion.

When Grandma heard my news it was decided that she, Grandpa, and I would have our own slumber party. She said we would have more fun than those other girls and that I would forget all about them. Grandma was right. Their slumber party had been cancelled due to the blizzard and ours was in full swing. Grandma was teaching me how to cook goulash, Grandpa was preparing to sing some of our favorites, and my dissatisfaction with having been left out had all but vanished.

"Who is Clarence Howe?" I finally said.

Grandma leaned over my shoulder and turned the flame down under the pan, smiling at my impatience with both the goulash and the discussion.

"He was a farmer your grandpa and I knew when your mother was just a baby. He wandered away in a blizzard and froze to death," she said, the flawless skin of her brow furrowing slightly with the gruesomeness of the recollection.

"How did that happen?" I asked, morbid fascination spurring my inquisitiveness.

Noticing something on the floor, Grandma bent to pick up the broken guitar string that Grandpa had overlooked, and missed the disapproving shake of his head. Grandpa's deeply seated tenderness caused him to wince at the tragedies of the world. Grandma on the other hand, although not without sentiment, approached things with a more blunt matter-of-fact style.

"During big snow storms like this, the power lines would blow down. It's pretty dark out on a farm with no light and snow flying everywhere. Well, anyway, Clarence had a barn full of milk cows to be fed and watered and he needed to get out there, despite the storm. His wife said that he tied an old rope around his waist and hooked it to the house thinking that if he couldn't find his way to the barn he wouldn't get lost in the blizzard. But the rope was rotted and it broke. It was horribly cold and he probably didn't feel it give way. He must have been a little numb. The kerosene lamp his wife sat in the kitchen window didn't shed enough light through all that falling and blowing snow for him to find his way back, either. He wandered around for quite a while and by that time he was so far from the house and so cold and tired from hyperthermia that he collapsed."

Grandpa, finished with the restringing, took his guitar into the dining room and began tuning it without comment. The wind howled under the eaves of the old house and rattled the storm gutters. The eerie sound evoked the image of a restless ghost, his eyes open wide and frost shrouding his frozen face, a frayed rope dangling from his waist as he clawed at the windows and doors of my imagination with his icy fingers. Did his restless spirit wander, looking for the light and warmth that he still thought could save him? I imagined the loneliness of being lost in the dark, the frigid whiteness blanketing the view of a kerosene lamp in the window and the moon and the stars hidden behind a thick gray cloud blanket. The thought chilled me even as my grandmother opened the oven door to retrieve the loaf of bread and a rush of hot air wrapped around my body. The soft notes of Grandpa's guitar drifted from the living room, bringing the fond memories of summer with them: the scent of wood smoke rising from a camp fire, the taste of a hotdog roasted over the flames, its exterior cracked and almost black, and the lap of waves against the stony shores of Marble Beach, mingled with lyrics about trains, magic dragons, and unrequited love, as my mind fused past with present and Clarence Howe's ghost vanished into the blizzard.

Later that night, when I nestled under the many quilts and blankets of the single metal bed beneath the dormered ceiling of a tiny second floor room that had once been my mother's , the specter reappeared. Each squeak of the old bedsprings, each crack and pop that the frigid temperature manifested from the wood framed house, each breath in the chilly darkness that seemed to belong to someone other than me, caused my ears to strain in hopes that I would recognize the source of the sound and the rapid thudding in my chest would slow. The clock on the night stand read 3:00 a.m., and I twisted fitfully, trying to rationalize my childish fear. I told myself that perhaps the ghost of Clarence Howe, if he truly existed, wasn't in search of the living because he desired to frighten them, but because he was lonely. Maybe he was misunderstood and only wanted the companionship that he had not had at the moment of his death. I unclenched my sweaty fists and remembered what my mother had said about fear, when, two days earlier, I had cried in her arms, questioning why my classmate disliked me enough to exclude me from her party.

"It's not because the girls don't like you," she had soothed, stroking my long dark hair and whispering the words like a lullaby into it, leaning protectively over my bowed head.

I had not felt reassured. An incident on the playground weeks earlier had been fresh in my mind.

"Don't play with Amy. She has diabetes and if you get too close to her, you'll catch it. Then you'll have to stick big needles in your arm every day!" one of the girls from my class had announced to the others who clustered around her at the teeter totter when I approached.

"You're wrong," I had sobbed."They hate me!"

Their screams and giggles still rang in my ears as they ran from me, the humiliation of their rejection still burned my cheeks, remembering my retreat to the monkey bars, where I had spent the remainder of recess alone, despising and envying the girls who avoided my glares from across the playground.

"They don't understand and it makes them afraid. It's not just the kids; it's their parents, too. I spoke with Patti's mom last week and she was concerned about your diabetes. She was afraid you might eat the wrong foods or that you might have a low blood sugar episode."

"But, Mom ...," I had protested, indignant that Pattie's mother thought I was so fragile and freakish that a simple slumber party would end in chaos if I was in attendance.

"I know. I know. But sometimes people can't let go of their fears, even when they're given the facts. I tried, Ames. I even offered to check in every hour, but she had already made up her mind."

"That's crap!" I had yelled, after assessing how foul of a word the situation would allow me to get by with.

"Yes, I agree. I think it's bullshit!"

My mother's more adult commentary on the situation had caused me to giggle through my tears, surprised by her outburst. She rarely cursed in front of me and I had realized by her unusual verbiage, that, she too, was frustrated with their stubborn ignorance.

My mother's words would stay with me through the remaining trials of childhood and into the difficult years of my adulthood, making me aware, time and again, that, too often, it was other's apprehensions that I would be forced to overcome.

Swinging my thin bare legs from beneath the cumbersome quilts, I stood, letting the flannel gown fall to the tops of my feet. I pulled back the filmy white curtain from the window and peered at the yard below. The storm had ended and the moon hung low and luminous over a sparkling landscape of curling snowdrifts and stark trees, their naked limbs reaching into the night sky like ancient fingers towards a gleaming pearl. As I watched, held by the beauty of the world beyond, an amazing scene unfolded. From a grove of trees across the road, rabbits began to appear, gathering on my grandparents' snowy lawn. The blizzard now over, free to leave the safety of their burrows, they leaped high into the air, chasing one another, dancing joyfully in the moonlight. Their celebration, although only a few moments in length, was marked with an audacity uncommon to their kind.

A cataract-like film of clouds soon covered the moon's brightness and the rabbits returned into the grove's thickening darkness, leaving behind a thousand tiny footprints, the story of their gathering written in a script no longer understood by most of humanity. A gust of wind suddenly covered the tracks and I, closing my eyes, made a silent wish that wherever Clarence Howe was this night, he had found peace.

CHAPTER FOUR

SUMMER OF THE MAGIC MOCCASINS

"You folks must be on vacation."

My mother set the bag of ice and the diet sodas on the counter and handed the gas station attendant a five dollar bill.

"Yes," she said, smiling wanly at his friendliness.

"Well, have a safe trip and enjoy your summer," he replied.

I took the paper bag from the counter, glancing at the cashier. I liked his tan face, lined with age. He wore a grease-stained work shirt with an oval patch that said "Pete" and tuffs of his gray hair stuck from beneath a faded red Phillips 66 cap. Like my father, he had the over-worked hands of a mechanic, rough and cracked, and when he caught me looking at him, he winked.

"I have a granddaughter about your age. Her mom and dad are taking her and her brothers out to Yellowstone this summer. Have you ever been to Yellowstone, young lady?"

I shook my head.

"Well, maybe your parents can take you next year. It's a beautiful place. You'd like it there."

My mother thanked him and we headed towards the blue hatchback where my father waited in the passenger's seat, staring through his dark wrap-around sunglasses at the cars exiting the interstate. When we were out of earshot, I turned to my mother.

"Why did you tell him we were on vacation?"

"I don't know. Maybe because I wish we were."

"I do, too."

Our exchange ended at the car door along with any fantasies of family getaways. Mom poured the ice into the cooler and I arranged the fruit, sandwiches, and sodas in the melting chips.

"Make sure those stay dry. We can't stop or your dad will be late for his appointment."

Her real concern for the food wasn't about lack of time, but rather the lack of money. Wrapping the plastic more tightly around the three bologna sandwiches, I balanced them against the soda cans, out of danger, and kept my thoughts about our cold lunch and our tight budget to myself. She pulled out into the flow of traffic and turned the Chevy towards the sign reading "Rochester 63 Miles". Dad said nothing, adjusting the visor against the harsh July sun. I stared at the southern Minnesota corn fields whizzing past as the hot humid air rushed through the open car window. Soon, the oppressive heat, the 4-cylinder engine's whine, and the need for escape drew me into daydreams of better summers and happier travels.

Several seasons earlier, before I had started Kindergarten, before I was diagnosed with diabetes, and before my father had begun to experience the physical implications of the disease, we had driven to South Dakota. My parents, my youngest uncle, Andy, and I rode for hundreds of miles in the old Chevelle, sweat and excitement pouring off us as the huge billboards flanking the highways promised oasis of exciting family attractions, colorful souvenirs, and clean, air conditioned lodging. The land the Lakota held sacred and had, a century earlier, defended against American invasion had become a hodge-podge of tourist traps, over-grazed ranch land, and monuments built by and for the conquerors. But the rows of rubber tomahawks and plastic headdresses lining the shelves of Wall Drug, the glass prisons that held snakes and lizards at the Reptile Gardens, and the monstrous pallid faces of Mount Rushmore could not diminish the power that emanated from the rocks of the Bad Lands and traveled on the wind that rustled the Black Hills pine. I felt a kind of inexplicable cellular memory flowing through my veins and feeding my bones, wordlessly connecting me to the power of the place and the history of its people.

The last evening of our vacation, my father stopped at a motel on the outskirts of Hill City. Dusty and road-weary, we welcomed the sight of the neon sign advertising "Kitchenettes, Color TV, and Swimming Pool". Andy soon discovered that the pool was drained except for a foot of very muddy water at its bottom and that the color TV only received one fuzzy channel, but the kitchenette contained an old refrigerator to keep my dad's insulin cool and a small stove for mom to cook some hamburgers. Andy threw his lanky body down on the worn sofa, propping his feet at one end and admiring his prized souvenir purchase, a pair of brown, fringed Minnetonka moccasins.

"Hey, Sis, pretty nice, huh?"

Mom smiled at her brother sprawled on the couch like a hippy god, his long brown hair hanging loose beneath his red bandana and his tie-dye T-shirt untucked from a pair of frayed denim cutoffs.

"You're cool," she said, rolling her eyes and giving him a thumbs-up.

I looked up at him for a second from the center of the double bed where I sat cross legged, thinking everything about my teen uncle, as I always did, was very cool. Then I returned my attention to a book's glossy photographs. My parents had allowed me to choose only one souvenir and I had mulled over the decision for a long time, finally selecting the book. Each page contained a photo of a different Lakota in his or her dance regalia. There were young men, their movement captured by the camera, with their long fringes flying and their knees bent high in the steps of the Grass Dance. There were beautiful women with shiny metal jingles adorning their elaborate dresses, and little girls, no older than I, wearing fancy hair ornaments made of beads and feathers. As I turned the pages, the images seemed to leap from the paper and I touched them, almost expecting that I would feel the softness of the buckskin or the smoothness of the bright beadwork against my fingertips.

Taking a second glance at my uncle's new moccasins, I flipped back to my favorite shot at the front of the book. A man and woman stood posed; both wore expressions of great pride and dignity. Streaks of gray lined the woman's hair and she held an eagle feather fan to her breast, her fringed dress hanging elegantly against her erect frame. The man, slightly younger, but just as austere as his companion, wore a large bustle of feathers, tanned leggings, and moccasins, the likes of which I had never seen. Hundreds of tiny colored beads, light blue, dark blue, white and yellow, formed geometric patterns across the top of his foot. The camera's lens had captured each shiny diamond, circle, and triangle as the light reflected off the cut glass, making them appear magical and alive. My uncle's new moccasins with their evenly machine-cut fringe and manufactured insoles didn't look anything like them. They did not have that enchantment.

Sitting spellbound, I rubbed my hands against the nubby chenille bedspread until my palms grew hot. Andy came over and sat down beside me, picking up my book and thumbing through the photographs. I laid my fingers on his arm.

"Why are your hands so warm?"

I put my palms back on the bed and demonstrated.

"Ah, yes," he smiled."Friction."

"Fiction?"

"No," he laughed."Friction. That's when two objects are rubbed together and it creates heat. I learned how to start a fire by using friction. If you take a stick and a rock and turn the stick really fast between your hands, the end of the stick will rub against the rock and make a spark. That's how everybody had to make fire before people had lighters and matches."

"Do you think if I rubbed my hands on the bedspread really fast I could start it on fire?"

He laughed again, swatting my head with the book before returning to the couch.

"We better keep an eye on the weather," my dad said, leaning closer to the grainy picture on the television screen as he tried to hear the news anchor's voice through the static.

Mom drew open the curtains and we looked out. The sky was black and ominous, clouds swirling across the horizon, the low rumble of thunder moving closer. My father abandoned the television's bad reception, opened the motel room door, and stepped outside to determine the direction of the storm. Wind picked up silt and sand, sculpting dirt devils and twisting them across the parking lot. I moved closer to the doorway and my mother warned me to stay inside, but I was drawn to the energy that crackled in the air and connected with my nerve endings. Jagged lightning spears cut through the darkness, hitting the ground with deafening crashes as torrents of rain sent my father running for the door. He grabbed my arm and pulled me inside.

"A tornado could drop out of this," he said."At the very least, some hail."

I stared at the spectacle beyond the window with a mixture of apprehension and awe, as another bolt of lightning tore across the blackness, illuminating my wide-eyed face.

Friction.

The sky is rubbing against the earth. It's alive. It's magic.

In the distance, the horizon turned pea green and the wind and rain subsided. Hail pellets began to fall, growing larger and more numerous, pelting the motel roof like a thousand dancing feet. Again, I felt the power of the land. It was above me. It was around me. It was inside of me. I closed my eyes and imagined the hail as a cleansing, rather than a destructive, force. Maybe it would erase the dead faces of Mount Rushmore from the Black Hills. Perhaps it would smash the glass aquariums, freeing the reptiles from the man-made garden. When the storm had passed, the rubber tomahawks would have disappeared along with a million pairs of factory produced moccasins.

For reasons I couldn't explain, the thought of the purification soothed me and I smiled as I watched the hail splash into the swimming pool's sludge. Later, when the storm was over and everyone was asleep, I lay awake and focused on the vacancy sign's hypnotic blink between the slightly parted curtains. At the end of the sofa, in a disappearing and reappearing shaft of weak red light, lay my uncle's moccasins, lifeless and artificial. I had turned my back to them, clinging to the hope that mysticism still existed in the world.

Plunged headlong into the present moment, the memory of South Dakota blurred, then faded, as my mother drove to the entrance of the Mayo Clinic. We had arrived early and she took the sandwiches and soda from the back seat while Dad and I walked to a bench under a cedar tree.

My father, quiet and tense, declined the sandwich, saying that he wasn't hungry. With her prodding, I made a half-hearted attempt to eat, but the bread tasted stale and the bologna greasy. I tossed it into a trash can when they weren't looking. The decision more than likely would lead to a low blood sugar episode later in the day, but I didn't care. Annoyed with us both, my mother discarded the rest of her lunch as well and I followed my parents, as they walked, without speaking, into the clinic.

When my father's name was called and he had solemnly gone from the waiting room, I saw the familiar lines on my mother's face, the ones that seemed to be there more often than not.

"It's bad this time, isn't it?" I said.

She didn't make eye contact as she spoke."He has a large hemorrhage. There is a clot of blood that is blocking all but some of his side vision in the left eye."

"Is Dad going blind?"

She dried her palms on her pant leg."The doctor thinks that if the laser treatments are successful, the bleeding will stop and the clot will eventually clear out. It's still a very new procedure, so we need to keep our fingers crossed. Your Dad's been really worried that if he loses his sight, he won't be able to go back to work, that he won't be able to take care of us."

"What would happen then? Would you have to get another job?"

"Yes, we couldn't get by on what I earn now. You'd have to help out more at home, too. We all would just have to do ...."

She stopped, shook her head, and frowned."No, there's no reason to talk about this now. We will deal with it when and if it comes. He's going to be all right. We're all going to be all right. No matter what happens, we'll get by."

I nodded and she patted my arm. I had other questions about my father's hemorrhages, but agitation about the possible answers halted my asking. In the weeks before our trip to Rochester, I had overheard my parents discussing my father's diabetes and the need to gain better blood sugar levels. They had spoken of something called "retinopathy" and his recent visit to the eye doctor brought the realization that diabetes had damaged his vision. Later, in my room, I had dug the booklets that I had been given at the time of my own diagnosis from the closet. Too little at the time to read the big words, I had ignored the material, but now, fully capable of understanding the medical verbiage, my breath caught in my chest as I turned to the back of the first pamphlet.

In a section marked "Possible Ramifications of Type I Diabetes," I learned Dad's and my potential fates."Heart Disease," "Amputations," "Kidney Failure," and "Blindness" screamed through my brain like warning sirens. Although I knew that both my father and I were at risk, the threat seemed more imminent for him. I could not imagine myself, a child who had only lived with the disease for a few years, having a limb amputated or having a heart attack. I rationalized that diabetic children were exempt from that kind of loss. But my father, on the other hand, had had diabetes working its destruction on his body for over twenty years.

Is he losing his eyesight? Is my father going blind? Maybe diabetic children do have heart attacks. Maybe diabetic children go blind. What if both of us lost our sight or our legs?

Suddenly, the thoughts stole my composure and I choked, tears welling, my temples pounding. I threw the booklets and pamphlets into the corner of the closet, causing the pages to tear loose from the staples and sending paper flying like the feathers of a bird that has flown into something large, invisible, and deadly. Pressing my back against the wall, I pulled my legs to my chest, rocked, and cried, my face buried in my knees. Later, when I calmed, I collected the pages from among the sneakers, stuffed animals, and board games, and hid them on the book shelf, between the Nancy Drew mysteries. Without mentioning what I had learned about our shared illness, I went to my father, while he sat in his favorite easy chair. I wrapped my arms around his neck. He wore the brave face he always wore when he wanted to convince everyone, especially me, that he wasn't worried, wasn't scared, wasn't in pain. Kissing his cheek, I slid the face on, too.

When Dad returned to the waiting room, he was holding the nurse's arm and wearing a patch behind his dark glasses. We stood and she transferred my father's hand to Mom's elbow.

"You will have to assist him, Mrs. Krout. The doctor treated both eyes this visit. The right one is dilated."

She explained the doctor's instructions to my mother, before bidding us farewell.

"Do you want to sit for a minute, Merle?" my mother asked.

He exhaled, his voice low and monotone."I just want to get out of here."

Moving towards the elevators, I glanced at him. His steps were tentative and unnatural and he stayed close to Mom, trying to conceal his dependency on her from people we passed in the hall. The ghost white edges of the eye patch shown just beyond the frames of his glasses. Again, my pulse beat hot in my head and my stomach clenched, but I kept the tears at bay and swallowed the rising acid.

We rode like three strangers, speeding along I-90, headed towards the blinding sun burning on the western skyline, each of us longing for the safety of home. Mom squinted behind the visor at the storm clouds banking up on the horizon in her rearview mirror and pressed the accelerator down, focused on reaching Mankato before the rain caught up. Either asleep or deep inside his own thoughts, my father didn't speak.

Exhausted from the heat, I passed in and out of dreams where doctors and nurses in white lab coats circled, knives, saws, and hatchets poised above me. I woke, startled, before sleep drug me under once more and I found myself alone in the Bad Lands, prairie dogs scurrying away from my intrusion. I followed them, hungry and despondent, hoping that I would be welcomed if I could prove myself harmless. But as I approached, they darted into their holes, vanishing beneath the barren surface of the land. The man with the magic moccasins approached, holding a bologna sandwich and I accepted it, grateful for the food. I looked at his feet, the beauty of the beaded designs lulling me into a sense of security, until he took my face in his hands and turned it towards his. Bowing his head, he revealed a clean white eye patch against his copper skin. Drops of blood ran from under it like a trail of scarlet tears. Again, I jerked awake, my skin clammy, my hands shaking. The car had stopped and my mother looked concerned, touching my forehead and then my hand.

"You're having a low blood sugar, aren't you?"

Although I heard what she was saying, it didn't make sense and I shook my head. Little trickles of cold sweat ran down my neck and my arms and legs trembled.

"Eat this!" She shoved a caramel into my mouth. Everything was spinning and my jaw felt too weak to chew the candy.

"Eat it, Amy! You need some sugar. Come on. Help me here. You're going to pass out. Chew, damn it!"

Her pleas broke through the hypoglycemic fog and I started to swallow the lump of melted caramel. I gagged, then forced it down. Dad fumbled to open a Tootsie Roll wrapper, finally peeling the sticky paper from it and shoving it in my direction. I took it, holding it tightly in my sweaty fist, but still too confused to know that I needed to eat it. Grabbing it, Mom stuck it in my mouth. They worked with the precision of paramedics; my father digging in the glove box, retrieving butterscotch drops, caramels, and peppermints from our emergency stash, while my mother ripped the paper free and administered the medicine.

"I'm sorry," I began to sob."I'm so sorry. I didn't mean for this to happen."

"It's all right. Don't cry. It's fine. We'll go inside and have a hot dinner and wait the storm out."

Wiping the tears on my T-shirt, I saw that we were parked at a restaurant. The wind picked up and a tumble weed blew across the car hood, landing at the feet of a giant statue of a grinning chef.

"Are you ready to go inside? Do you feel better?" she asked.

I nodded and we piled from the car as the first drops of rain fell. She grabbed Dad's arm and guided him towards the door, his face reddening as he stumbled over the curb. He swore under his breath. Despite our rush, we were drenched. Feeling as disheveled and bedraggled as we looked, we fell into a booth, our mood as soggy as our clothes. I scanned the laminated menu's photographs of meat loaf with brown gravy, waffles and link sausages, and apple pie a la mode, while trying to ignore the one-sided argument that was unfolding across the table.

"I am doing the best I can, Merle. I didn't see that curb. No one saw you trip."

His jaw tightened with every word, until finally he slapped the menu down on the table and turned towards my mother, looking as if he might cry.

"I don't want to talk about it," he finally said, emotion seeping through the control.

The waitress arrived, temporarily breaking the tension, so I ordered a cheeseburger and fries from the kids' menu, wanting something as normal as a hot meal to batten down everything that seemed to be flying apart. But the caramels, Tootsie Rolls, and butter scotch drops sat like a stone in my stomach, and when the food arrived, it looked completely unappetizing to me. Beside our booth, the view beyond the plate glass window blurred as the rain came in sheets. From across the restaurant, another child's laughter blended with the hum of amiable adult conversation and I watched my parents, mechanically eating in their silent separate worlds. Suddenly, I couldn't swallow what was in my mouth and I shot out of the booth, cupping my hand over my lips and bolting towards the restroom. Alarmed, my mother sprang from her seat and chased after me. When I reached the stall, I dropped on my knees at the commode, purging everything I no longer could bear: my father's frustration, his vision of the future obscured by an unknown fate, my mother's fatigue, her patience and faith stretched so thin, the shadows of anger and doubt shown through, and my sadness at the very real probability that *my* family would never see Yellowstone.

CHAPTER FIVE

SPRING OF THE ZINNIA

The vibrant green blades of grass stood in contrast to the rich black earth at the edge of my mother's garden where she knelt, shoulders stooped, carefully sowing a handful of tiny seeds. I kicked off my sandals, thrilling at the sensation of the prickly spring shoots that tickled the soles of my bare feet. The long months of wool socks and winter snow boots had left my feet pale and tender and I walked several steps, my body reacquainting itself with the feel of the grass. Looking up from her planting, my mother grinned at the little hops, twists, and cartwheels I performed around the old rusty swing set under the walnut tree.

"Come and help me. I'm putting the marigolds in," she said, brushing aside a strand of long brown hair.

I trotted back to the garden's edge and rolled the legs of my jeans up before crossing from the lush green lawn into the moist soil. Like the grass, the dirt felt new and wonderful and I dug my toes into its rich dampness.

"You can start covering the seeds I have in the row," she said, "but don't bury them too deep and don't pat the soil down on top of them. We don't want to make it too difficult for them to sprout."

I followed my mother's direction, squatting and pushing small handfuls of earth into the shallow furrow. One of the seeds stood out from the rest and I stopped to examine it.

"This one is different. Is it a marigold, too?" I asked, lifting the dark oval seed from the ground and holding it up for her to see.

She squinted at it in the afternoon sunshine before reaching her hand out. I placed the seed in her palm, anxious to know from which flower it came.

"I believe this is a zinnia," she said, turning it between her thumb and forefinger.

She stood, moving towards the other side of the garden where a wicker basket filled with seed packets sat.

"I'll put this with the other zinnias."

"No!" I said, my concern over the zinnia seed's fate surprising my mother as well as myself.

She turned and raised her eyebrows quizzically.

"What do you think we should do with it?"

"I think we should plant it here with the marigolds," I said, holding my hand out.

"All right," she replied, and returned the seed, resisting the urge to question the logic of a nine-year-old.

"Maybe it's a zinnia on the outside but a marigold on the inside and that's why it wants to live with the other marigolds," I said, laying the dark seed beside the lighter ones in the row and filling in the rest of the furrow with earth.

"I suppose that's possible," she said, her pretty brown eyes sparkling with amusement.

She carried a large wooden flat of pepper and tomato plants to the north end of the garden.

"Can I help plant those, too?" I asked, suddenly remembering that I was supposed to be doing something else, something that I did not exactly want to do.

"Sure," she said."I always appreciate your help."

Her enthusiasm sparked a tinge of guilt and I hesitated, knowing that she would be disappointed at the reason I chose to linger in the garden. Dragging a bundle of wire cages closer to the area where the peppers and tomatoes were to be planted, I reluctantly addressed my mother.

"When we finish putting these in, do you think we could go over to Grandpa and Grandma's?"

She set the box of small pepper plants back into the wooden crate and narrowed her gaze at me, the realization of the situation hitting her. I looked away as my cheeks grew red.

"So that's what this is all about. I knew there was something you were supposed to do this afternoon. You better get going. Your project isn't going to finish itself."

I raked my bare toes through the grass, still not looking directly at her. She was right. My third grade teacher had assigned the genealogy project two weeks ago and it was due tomorrow. Initially, I had been excited about my genealogical exploration, creating a painted tree with numerous shades of green leaves formed by dabbing the huge sheet of poster paper with different shapes of sponge, drawing the carefully ruled lines among the brown offshoots that extended upward from the massive trunk and would contain the names of my ancestors, and practicing with the calligraphy pen with which I intended to record the family lineage. I had peddled the four short blocks to my Grandpa and Grandma Clark's house, eager to fill my tree's many branches. The anticipation of its growth had increased as I collected names, stories, and memories that stretched the width of the Atlantic and kindled for me a new fascination with England, Scotland, and Germany. But as I tucked the blue notebook containing the history of my mother's family into my bicycle basket and rode down my grandparent's gravel drive, I had noticed an old elm that stood apart from the evergreens across the road. A large section of the tree was covered in leaves and light green buds, but the side that was not as visible from the road was bare. The branches hung twisted and sickly in the deepening shadows of early evening. Only a few stunted leaves fluttered from the diseased portion of the tree and I had shivered, remembering that I had completed only half of the journey into my family's past.

"Will you please come with me, Mom," I pleaded, as I watched my mother dig a hole with a hand trowel and place a pepper plant in it.

"Why is this so difficult for you?"

"I don't know," I said, returning my gaze to my feet.

But I did know. The knowledge lay shrouded in the memory of an image, an image that told the story more clearly than words ever could. As I stood at the edge of the garden staring at my feet, it again told its tale in my mind.

Grandma Ann had removed her shoes, preparing to go to bed. I had been five years old and had not been able to stop myself from gasping when I saw the terrible sight. Her toes were crippled, gnarling into a grotesque bunch at the ends of her feet. She had pulled off the numerous pads, bandages, and wadded cotton she used to try to make her shoes more comfortable before she noticed the look on my face and had quickly slid on a pair of slippers in order to shield me from her deformity. Without my asking, she had explained, her voice hushed, as if she were telling a secret.

"When I was a little girl, I never had shoes that fit properly. We were only allowed to take them off during baths and at bedtime. My feet got bigger. My shoes did not."

I suddenly had felt afraid and I slid closer to my grandmother on the bed where we sat. I looked up at her face. She looked old and very tired, and although my shoulder rested against the arm of her housecoat, there seemed to be a great distance between us. She stared for many moments at her reflection in the mirror that hung above the dresser, her eyes so lonely and sad that I tugged gently at her sleeve, wanting to retrieve her from the thought that held her in its grasp. Another moment had passed before she closed her eyes to the old woman she saw in the glass, wrapping a frail arm around me and hugging tightly. I had wiggled my bare toes beneath the hem of my robe, trying to free the image of my Grandma Ann's ruined feet along with the many questions I had about her explanation from my mind, as we lingered in the soothing comfort that only exists in silence.

"Growing up wasn't easy for Grandma Ann or Grandpa Jack," my mother said, stirring the peaceful hush that hung over the garden and interpreting the meaning behind my hesitancy with her words.

I nodded, encouraged by her understanding and by the outside chance that her knowledge would lead her to join me at my grandparent's house.

She shoveled dirt around a tomato plant and motioned for a cage to put over it. I handed her the wire support and watched her position it so that the fragile green stalk would have a place to climb as it grew. She continued to work as she spoke.

"They don't talk much about their lives before your dad and Uncle Roger were born. I think there are a lot of bad memories for them. They both lost their parents when they were quite young and were separated from their sisters and brothers. Your Grandpa Jack's father abandoned his children. I don't know much about his mother."

"That's why I don't want to do this, Mom. I don't want to make them talk about things that are going to make them sad. I love them," I said, feeling a dry tightness forming in my throat.

"I know that and they know it, too, Ames. They probably won't have many stories to tell you, but I'm sure they will share with you what they do know about your ancestors."

Peeling off her faded gardening gloves, my mother put a hand on my shoulder.

"You can do this by yourself. I have confidence in you. Not everything worth learning in life is going to come easy. This is one of those things. The stories that your grandparents have about the family's past aren't all happy, but they're not all sad, either. Those memories and the people in them are the ingredients of who your grandma and grandpa are. They are the ingredients of who you are, too. The more you know about them, the more you will know about yourself."

She wiped a smudge of earth from my cheek and kissed my forehead.

"Now go wash up. I have to get moving. There's a few hours of daylight left and I want to weed the raspberry bed before dark."

When I departed, the sun was shining through a stand of evergreens that fringed the west edge of the yard, the weakening rays falling across my mother's back. She lovingly lowered the last tomato plant into the earth, and, as she did with every plant, every bulb, every seed, she offered a prayer. I stopped for a moment, looking at the row where the zinnia seed lay hidden just below the surface somewhere amongst the future marigold flowers. For one anxious moment, I fought back the overwhelming urge to fall to my knees and sift through the loose soil in search of the black oval seed. I wanted to return it to the paper packet marked "zinnia". How could I have been so wrong? It should be with its own kind. Perhaps it could not survive if left to grow surrounded by flowers so much smaller and frillier than itself. I stepped towards the garden and then hesitated, realizing I was not sure that the row I was looking at actually contained flowers at all. Maybe it was a row of carrots or the green beans that I loved so much. I could not be sure. My mother always planted flowers and vegetables together. She liked the beauty and color that the blooms created between the vivid green vegetable plants and the natural insect repellent some of the flowers provided.

Knowing that I could not risk destroying the many hours of labor she had devoted to planting by inadvertently plunging my fingers into the wrong section of seeds, I turned and climbed the grassy hill to the outdoor faucet. As the icy water splashed over my hands and feet, I told myself that the zinnia would be all right. Surely it didn't matter whether it grew among the marigolds. It would still be a zinnia regardless of its surroundings or the other plants that lived beside it. Rubbing my hands dry on my pant leg, I put on my sandals and gazed across the narrow road towards my destination. Grandpa Jack sat in an old lawn chair on the front porch, waving.

Yes, a zinnia is still a zinnia no matter where it grows.

CHAPTER SIX

SPRING OF BLEEDING HEARTS

Grandpa Jack and Grandma Ann lived an unsurprising life. My grandfather drank his coffee from the same stained white ceramic mug each morning and ate corn flakes from the same blue cereal bowl. Each afternoon, he would walk to the post office, occasionally stopping at Chuck's Tavern to socialize with the other local retired men. On Fridays he drove his late model Ford to the gas station to top off the fuel, washed the car in the driveway with a bucket of soapy water and a garden hose, and took my grandma on errands. Grandma Ann's days were allotted to domestic chores: Tuesday was laundry day, she vacuumed and dusted on Thursday, and Friday was reserved for a trip to the grocery store, where the same brand of soap, the same flavor of ice cream, and the same cuts of meat were purchased. Every Saturday afternoon, she washed her hair and set it with rollers and pin curls before sitting under an old hair dryer while manicuring her nails. She attended church each Sunday while my grandfather stayed home and read the newspaper. They moved through the years in a comfortable and predictable groove, their steps only altering slightly with the change of seasons. But despite the fact that I always could find a half of a stick of Doublemint in her purse or that he would always have a pack of Kent cigarettes in his breast pocket, my grandparents remained a mystery to me.

I pondered the many unanswered questions I harbored about their lives as I walked through the shadows cast by the box elders that lined the circular drive in front of their house. Who was the woman I knew I would find, small and unobtrusive, in the kitchen preparing the evening meal? Who was this man I saw sitting on the porch? His straight gray hair brushed back from his forehead, his deep-set hazel eyes brightening as I mounted the wooden steps.

"Hi, Grandpa," I said, putting my arms around his neck, breathing in the scent of Aqua Velva and tobacco smoke.

"Little One," he said, calling me the pet name that only he used.

His lips curled in a slight smile as he stood, folding the lawn chair and propping it against the porch railing. The detachment that his face so often registered disappeared momentarily when I was present, letting the subtle hints of his love and pride show through the usual expressionless mask that guarded his heart from the rest of the world.

"Grandma's going to help me with my school project. I have to do a family tree for class," I said, the blue notebook suddenly cumbersome in my sweaty hands.

Grandpa Jack didn't say anything as he opened the screen door for me, but I could not help noticing that the brightness had faded from his eyes and the smile was gone from his mouth. The protective mask had reappeared. Grandma was in the kitchen as I expected, her back turned towards me, shoulders slumped, peeling potatoes into a dish pan. I sat down at the table and caught her profile in the last rays of sunlight that passed through the open window, illuminating her face and hands. She was beautiful, her eyes following the motion of a pair of red-breasted robins as they splashed and preened in the cracked cement bird bath just beyond the kitchen window. The tiny lines of worry, disappointment, and loss that had accumulated over the years softening, the happiness of the bathing bird's awakening the beauty within her face.

"You're pretty, Grandma."

She turned from the sink, blushing and shaking her head.

"You are a silly girl if you think your old granny is pretty," she said, refusing to accept my compliment and turning her attention back to the cooking.

The delicious aroma of roast beef floated from the oven and she dropped the potatoes in a pot of boiling water before she came and sat with me at the table.

"The roast smells great. You always make the best roast beef."

"Yes, that smell does make you hungry, doesn't it?"

She smiled then, this compliment somehow more acceptable to her than my last, and tapped the cover of the blue notebook with her index finger, her voice low and apologetic.

"I'll help you as much as I can with this, but there is an awful lot that I don't know about my family. There's an awful lot that I have forgotten. It's the same for Grandpa. We were both very young when we lost our folks and we didn't have much family around to take care of us or tell us about our people."

"That's all right. I don't have to make the tree very big. Just a couple of our relatives' names and maybe a story, if you want to tell me any. That's all I really need."

Opening the notebook, I doodled little clovers and hearts in the blank margins of the ruled sheet."Krout" was penciled at the top of the page and I erased it, rewriting it in capital letters, all the time hoping my words had provided a comfortable place somewhere between fact and fiction where Grandma Ann would feel safe in telling me her story. I could not admit how important the assignment really was or that our family tree would be exhibited among the genealogical projects of my classmates at the elementary open house at the end of the school year.

The many pages of names in the front of my book and the stories of my mother's ancestors that accompanied them would remain tucked out of sight. I didn't want her to feel pressured, inadequate, or ashamed of her childhood. She and my grandfather, like all children who have suffered the cruelties of abuse and neglect, were innocent victims, still, after decades, carrying scars, both visible and invisible. Grandma crossed her ankles under the chair and I glimpsed her misshapen feet, hidden by the worn brown lace-ups she always wore.

"I was born in South Dakota. My grandmother came from Germany and I lived with her for a while after my parents were gone. She only spoke German at home and, by the time I started school, my English wasn't very good."

Grandpa Jack rose from his usual chair in the living room and clicked the set on. Returning to his spot, he lit a cigarette and picked up the Lake Park News from the end table where the massive glass ashtray always sat, constructing layers of smoke, rustling newspaper, and muffled television jingles between him and the sound of Grandma's voice.

"We didn't have much in those days; course, no one did. It was during the Depression and times were tough for everyone. But we did all right. I remember my grandmother got us some chicks from a neighbor and we were going to raise them, some for laying eggs and some for frying. Money was scarce and we couldn't always afford feed, so we would throw the kitchen scraps out for them. They were doing well, eating the vegetable peels, but one day some sprouts from some potatoes got tossed with everything else and the little chicks couldn't swallow them."

Grandma leaned closer, her expression serious and determined, as she remembered how the fluffy yellow birds began to choke, some dropping dead at her feet, before her grandmother had rushed from the house with a kitchen knife in her hand.

"She slit open the gullets of the ones that hadn't died yet and took out the sprouts while I ran and got a sewing needle and thread. I stitched them up and we were able to save most of them. It was a good thing, too, because eggs and chicken were about all we had to eat that winter. Not real sure what we would have done otherwise."

Speechless, I sat staring at her, the scene playing and replaying over and over in my mind. I saw the old woman, wielding a kitchen knife and yelling desperate commands in German at a frightened young girl as she worked with steady hands, despite the immensity of the situation, to suture the gaping throats of the fragile struggling chicks. Why had my grandmother chosen to share this particular story? What about it affected me so much? On visiting my mother's parents, Grandma Bonnie, too, had told accounts involving the hardships of the Depression: the loss of my great grandfather's grocery store after he had extended credit to families who no longer had an income and how my grandmother and her sister sold homemade potato chips and roasted peanuts on the street to keep pennies in their pockets. I appreciated the ingenuity and tenacity that my Grandma Bonnie's story represented and derived a great sense of pride at learning of Great Grandfather Tott's generosity and selflessness, but it was the tale of my Grandma Ann's chickens that struck deeper into my core.

It was a subtle change in her posture, the way she suddenly seemed to be sitting a bit more erect against the back of the old wooden chair and the little lift in her chin that transformed her usual apologetic pose into one of modest, yet undeniable, triumph. I knew at that moment that her recollection had revealed much more than just her ability to survive the struggles of poverty. It was far more personal to her than that. In a childhood wrought with emptiness and disappointment, it was a pivotal moment, a moment where life had not conceded to death, loss had not been the predictable outcome as it had been so many times before, and for the first time, my grandmother's hands had helped in shaping her own fate. The chickens, at least for the moment, had escaped the cruel role of victim, and she, for once, had too.

I gazed down at the blank sheet of notebook paper, suddenly aware that I hadn't recorded her account of the chickens, but knowing I would never forget it. She told me the names of her grandmother, her parents, and her sisters, the only ones Grandma Ann could remember or, perhaps, had ever known and I penciled them across the empty lines. As I wrote, I stole furtive glances out of the corner of my eye at Grandpa Jack, who still sat concealed behind his newsprint fortress.

"Grandpa, can I ask you about your family?" I said, the pencil still poised.

Without moving the paper from in front of his face, he exhaled audibly from behind it, sending a gray cloud of smoke towards the ceiling.

"Ask your grandmother. She knows as much as I do."

Grandma threw a disapproving look in his direction, but didn't argue with his decision.

"Your grandpa was born here, in Iowa. His father ran off when he was quite young. He might have gone to Texas, if I remember correctly."

Grandpa remained silent, making no attempt to confirm or deny her recollection.

"Catholic boarding school. His mother sent him there. I'm not sure why, but it was a very bad place for a young boy. The nuns beat him. I think that is why your grandpa won't go to church with us. Too many terrible memories," she continued, whispering as if he must be protected from hearing the story of his own past.

"Why did they beat him? Was he naughty?"

It was hard for me to comprehend this kind of violence towards a child. I recalled having received only one spanking as a toddler, when I had run out into the street in front of a passing car after being told by my mother that I must never cross alone. The sting of the swat on my rear had long been forgotten, but I soon understood my mother's reaction as I grew and learned that it was love, not rage, that had fueled her. But Grandma did not say that the boarding school nuns had spanked or swatted my grandfather, they had beaten him. What had fueled them?

"No, I doubt your grandpa was a bad boy. His behavior probably didn't have a whole lot to do with it. They were always trying to beat something out of you or into you."

She slumped her shoulders and hung her head, cowering from the distant, yet not distant enough, nightmare of the many beatings she herself had endured.

"When they picked up that strap, or the ruler, or balled their fist, you always knew they were going to beat the sin out of you or the fear of God into you. More than likely, they saw something in your grandfather they just didn't like, something they couldn't accept."

"What did they see in him?"

"His parents were divorced and in those days, especially among Catholics, that was considered unacceptable, sinful. His mother remarried and lived in Sioux City. He certainly wasn't responsible for what his parents did, but I guess those nuns didn't see it that way. It's a shame how people punish children for what their parents do or for who their fathers are."

What do you mean? Who was grandpa's father?"

"He was an Indian."

Grandpa Jack stood in the kitchen doorway, one hand rested against the jam, the other still holding the crumpled newspaper. The potatoes boiled violently in their pot, thudding against the bottom and sides in their frantic dance and rattling the lid in ominous warning of their pending leap into the flames. My grandfather's eyes met mine and I saw the tiniest pinpoint of light flickering in the shiny black pupils, like the gleam of a star, its brilliance diminished only by the unfathomable space and time that exists between itself and Earth. Like the last spark of a long unattended and slowly dying fire, it held my gaze as his words traveled through my veins, planting their meaning at the center of my self.

"He was an Indian," he repeated, never unlocking his intense stare from my wide unblinking eyes, his voice a whisper in the dusky shadows that darkened his angular face.

"Are we Indians, Grandpa?"

He didn't seem to expect my question, and his eyes broke away from mine as he shoved his hand deep into the pocket of his faded blue jeans as if the answer lay somewhere amongst the loose change and balled up cigarette wrappers.

"I suppose some places we would be," he said, "but not here."

When he again looked in my direction, the light that had held me transfixed was gone and in its place lay the dull look of shame and regret. Shame, not for who he truly was, for brutality hadn't fully succeeded in bringing him to the complete denial of his father's blood, but the regret for never having been allowed to live it. Having passed the spark on to me, he now dreaded the consequences that might befall me because of the knowledge I carried. Did he see the apparition of a nun looming over me, strap in hand, prepared to extinguish the tiny light and beat the Indian blood from my thin body? Perhaps it was not the nuns, but the skills he had developed in order to survive in the larger society that caused him to declare his father's identity, while, at the same time, denying that he nor I were Indian. Survival had meant passing through the world unnoticed by those who might not want an Indian working on their farm or living next door. He had successfully "passed" throughout his adult life and I knew that he wanted me to do the same. It would be so easy, with my light skin and blue eyes, but time would reveal that my exterior exposed very little of my true identity as the spark I inherited slowly ignited over the years and became the roaring flames of a sacred fire.

Leaving my grandparent's house in the deepening twilight, he walked with me to the edge of the porch where he bent and, with a pocket knife, cut a stem of bleeding hearts from my grandmother's flower bed. He handed the fragile pink blooms to me and I held the arching green stalk between my thumb and forefinger, examining the seven dangling blossoms that hung in graduating sizes. Vibrant pink petals like the winged halves of a broken heart separated from each other, a translucent stamen protruding from between the separation. The three small hearts had not yet "bleed" and I ran my fingertip across them, silently wishing that they would be spared in ways that my grandparents had not.

"I'll walk you home, Little One," he said, grasping my free hand in his and nodding towards my father, who stood across the street on our back step with his empty lunchbox in his hand.

I glanced at the flowers several times as I walked beside Grandpa, wondering why they were named bleeding hearts. The exposed stamens really did not look like drops of blood at all, but, rather, like tears. As we crossed the empty street, I held onto Grandpa Jack's hand tighter, my mind flashing on him as a boy, his face stained with tears as he denounced his blood under the lash of a strap. I knew then that the name was right, for too often our blood brought our tears.

CHAPTER SEVEN

SUMMER OF SPLINTERS AND SPARKS

It was not unlike so many other July Sunday mornings. The robins and sparrows foraged on the back lawn, their sleek heads disappearing from view between the long blades of grass where the dew still clung. The scent of moist earth and green walnuts drifted through the open window on the balmy air. Somewhere, a bell tolled, summoning one flock or another to its respective fold. It was the slow and similar way most Sundays began in a small sleepy town like ours. But the anticipatory quickening of my pulse signaled a shift in the energy that flowed through our home and I, having set the changes in motion, anxiously waited for the inevitable rift to rip through the last lingering moments of tranquility. It was the day on which, for reasons I wanted to explain but did not yet have the words, I began to disentangle myself from the web of my Christian upbringing, one sticky thread at a time.

My eyes darted expectantly from the peaceful scene beyond the window to the locked door and thoughts unraveled in my head as I considered the decision I had made earlier, announcing at the breakfast table that I would not be going to church. When my mother had determined that I was not ill but simply had decided not to attend, she glared, her lips all but disappearing in a thin angry line.

"Does everything have to be a fight with you?" she asked, hurling the dish cloth into the sink, toppling the stack of ceramic bowls and stainless steel spoons with a nerve-jarring crash.

"No, I don't want to fight, but I don't want to go to church, either," I said, pushing the chair from the table, preparing to escape her wrath.

My father calmly drank his coffee, never looking in my direction, unwilling to take sides in the battle that was about to ensue. I went to my room and slammed the door, an action that I knew would further grate against my mother's nerves in more than one way. I had discovered a few years earlier that it was broken and if I used the appropriate amount of force it could only be unlatched from the interior of the bedroom, leaving the old brass knob to spin uselessly in the hand of anyone trying to enter from the hallway. The malfunction was a dangerous weapon in the control of a strong-willed girl like me and it had quickly become the bane of her existence. She had requested several times that my father fix it, but it was one task he hadn't gotten around to yet and so I shamelessly continued to use it to my advantage. Although the tightness in my belly had predicted its arrival, the sharp rapping at the door still startled me.

"You had better be getting ready for church, Amy Marie!"

The seriousness of the situation had escalated a notch with the addition of my middle name, but I did not respond, instead listening to the soft twitters of the robins that hunted and preened in the sunshine. Her angry footfalls briefly sounded in harsh juxtaposition to the faint whisper of the wind in the old cottonwood, before they faded down the hallway. I hunched cross-legged on the bed in my nightgown, hair disheveled as closets were opened and slammed, water ran in the bathroom sink, and muffled voices rose and fell.

"She is being difficult."

"What do you want me to do about it?"

"You should have fixed that door knob a long time ago."

I pressed my damp palms against the squares of the quilt piled beside me on the unmade bed. Grandma Ann had given it to me for my first birthday, each piece hand-sewn, each piece carefully cut from the discarded pairs of jeans, flannel shirts, cotton house dresses, and corduroy jackets that once had been worn by Grandpa Jack, Uncle Roger, my father, or her. It was a wonderful mixture of colors, designs, and textures and my finger stopped on the coarse tan wool that had once been part of my father's sport coat. As I stroked the worn fabric, I imagined him, slender and handsome, wearing it, his dark hair combed back, a mum corsage in his hand, a shy smile on his lips, nervously waiting for the Homecoming dance to begin. A tinge of guilt pricked my conscious, knowing that he was currently taking the heat for my silence. Again, my mother pounded, her fist causing the mirror on the wall to vibrate, the reflection of my face rippling on its surface. I flinched as she yelled her warning.

"You have exactly one minute to open this door. I have had enough! Do you hear me? Enough!"

I wanted to open the door. I wanted to reason with her. I wanted to explain to her that I wasn't pointlessly creating chaos, for it was not derived from the adolescent angst that usually provoked our arguments. But I knew it was too late for rational discussion and I wasn't sure I could assign words to the source of my resistance. All I knew with certainty was that the source was more powerful than her anger and far more convincing.

Tugging the quilt over my feet, I clutched it to my cheek, finding comfort and contemplation in the remnants of Uncle Roger's plaid flannel shirt and Grandpa Jack's brown corduroy pants. I thought of my grandfather, who I imagined, as he usually was on Sunday morning, across the street in his favorite chair, the Des Moines Register, his chosen gospel, open to the sports section and I wondered if the abusive nuns of his youth were the only catalyst in his distaste for Christianity. Perhaps he, too, felt the discontentment that I did when he sat inside the walls of "God's house". Had the words of the sermons, hymns, and prayers entered his head, like they did mine, never reaching the heart, and had he, too, left the church each Sunday with more questions than answers? Did my grandfather and I share a secret seed that lay dormant inside of our blood, unable to grow to fruition in the shadow of our religious upbringing or, like the shoes that had misshapen my grandmother's feet, was the church simply a haunting memory from his lost childhood?

The staccato click of high-heeled pumps against the wooden hallway issued their warning of my mother's approach and I cringed at the hollow echo of her fist on the door, more loud and violent than before.

"You will go to church," she screamed, "even if I have to break this damn door down. Do you hear me? I'll break it down!"

Had the standoff come from my usual poisonous mixture of diabetic mood swings and teenage rebellion, I would not have hesitated to point out the irony of her profanity, but my purpose wasn't to provoke her more than I already had, so I quietly huddled on the bed, my hands gripping the quilt like a shield. Her fists pummeled the door, and I wondered for a moment if she would make good on her threat of breaking it down, as her mounting fury revealed itself with each new blow to the old dry wood. My stomach knotted and I closed my eyes to the door quivering in its frame and my ears to the rattling of the knob and the thunder of her knocking. When I again opened my eyes, the door was still and my mother's screaming had ended. Unaware that the eerie stillness was but the passing eye of the storm, I unfolded myself from under the quilt's protection and approached the door. In the distance, the mournful tone of another church bell tolled and I hesitated, my fingers resting on the tarnished knob. Suddenly, the loud sickening crack of splintering wood followed by an agonized moan drowned out the bell's faint call to worship, and, gasping, I backed away from the horrible sound. She whimpered and stumbled into her room and I, concerned that she may have seriously injured herself, popped the latch to assess the damage. Ragged strips of glossy paper hung from the spot where a poster of the gender-bending pop star, Boy George, had once been, and a golf ball-sized hole now existed in the center of his brooding face, the wood cracked and splintered behind it. My mother sat on the edge of her bed, clutching her right foot and biting her lower lip. She looked up at me, her face crimson, and her voice shaking.

"I do not even want to look at you right now," she hissed, reaching for the scuffed black and white pump and shoving it back on her sore foot."I will deal with you later."

Wincing, she limped past me in the hallway and I followed at a safe distance, as she grabbed her purse and her Bible from the dining room table. The car idled in the driveway, my father impatiently revving the engine and she turned to face me, her hand gripping the handle of the screen door.

"Don't think for one second that this is over."

Our eyes locked for a long moment and I saw what was hidden behind her anger and frustration. She fought to conceal it, having played the role of defender against it throughout my childhood, but it was unmistakable. She was afraid.

Clutching the red leather Bible to her chest, she turned her gaze away from my unapologetic stare, no longer able to face the nameless thing that flickered defiantly in my blue eyes. The tenacious spark's origin was a mystery to her, for she and my father had carefully guided my spiritual journey thus far onto the path of Christianity. I had, as with so many things I had been presented with as a child, been unwilling to accept much of my religious education at face value and had asked more questions than my mother often felt comfortable with, but she hadn't expected my sudden opposition to it. Why did I now pull away from the only set of metaphysical beliefs with which she, my father, or I were familiar? At some point in time, between the moment in which the minister dampened my tiny dark head at the baptismal fount and this tumultuous morning fifteen years later, the tiny bright light had ignited and, although it was in constant threat of suffocation, sometimes growing very dim before finding fuel and regaining strength, it could not be extinguished. Perhaps if my mother had been sitting in my grandparents' kitchen on the day Grandpa Jack's eyes had harbored the same glimmering light, it would have been clearer to her.

Perhaps if she had witnessed the way in which his words and his gaze, holding the last ember of an ancient ancestral fire, had been given to his only granddaughter, she would recognize the secret, yet sacred, gift. But she was not there on that day when he spoke of his father and of being Indian. She hadn't seen that fleeting moment when his face had shone with defiant pride in our ancestry, only to slacken as the ghosts of his past caught up with him, reminding him of the sanctuary of silence and the safety of denial. She had not watched as he had crouched on tired old knees to cut the stem of bleeding hearts or to see the dejection in his eyes as he placed the fragile flowers in my hand.

My mother took another quick glance at me, shaking her head as if to detach my image and the confusion it conjured, before softly closing the screen door on the scene. Alone, I watched my parents drive down the quiet street, the hum of the engine fading behind them, the lullaby of the wind chimes swaying from the porch's overhang and the song of the cicadas, the only remaining music in the otherwise still morning. I sat on the cool concrete porch steps, elbows resting on knees, chin resting on palms, and considered my mother's parting words. It was not over. I knew it as well as she did.

The war raged on, both inside as well as outside of me for a long time. Battles would be lost as I sought, on some occasions, to please my family, sliding my body into the pew beside my mother, but allowing my heart, filled with ancient cellular memories of the sacred tobacco's sweet aroma and the power of forgotten chants, remembered with the blood rather than the mind, to carry my spirit far beyond the brick walls and stained glass. There, in a place that transcends space and time, it could wait, the glimmering light, the fragile seed, protected from a world that sought to destroy the gift of identity passed from my grandfather, through my father's blood, to me. As I grew older and the struggle to define my desire to seek a different path intensified, I, with the limited understanding and the conviction that I possessed, attempted to explain why, like Grandma Ann's girlhood shoes, I could not confine myself to a religion that, no matter how I tried, left my spirit cramped and crippled.

"If you aren't going to go to church and you don't accept the ideas in the Bible, what do you believe in? Are you an atheist?" my mother would demand, as our arguments over the years increased.

I was not an atheist. Of that fact, I could always assure her. But the question of my beliefs remained unanswered, for I had not yet learned the words to express what, at that time, could only live as a powerful feeling within my being. It was what filled me when the waves of Silver Lake lapped against Grandpa Lynn's canoe. It was the sight of the hidden seeds breaking through the earth in my mother's garden. It was the knowledge in the eyes of a blackbird. It was the fragility of a butterfly's wing. It was the sense of being part of rather than separate from or superior to, everything, seen and unseen, in the universe. And, as I sat, watching the Sunday morning unfold, I saw it in my grandfather.

After Grandma Ann's departure to join my parents at church, Grandpa Jack came out of the house into the side yard. He carried a bucket, which he stooped to fill at the outdoor faucet. As I observed from my vantage point, he carefully emptied the old cement bird bath and poured the clean water from the bucket into the bowl. Returning to the faucet, turning it on and letting it run until water splashed against his worn jeans, he then crossed the lawn to the small vegetable garden, carefully swinging a wide swath around the bird bath where several sparrows had landed and were enjoying the cool clear water. He began to pour the contents of his bucket along the row of carrots, but he stopped in the middle of the garden, the watering unfinished, his attention suddenly captured by something greater than his task. Tilting his face towards the sky, he put his hands in his pockets and stood very still, like one in prayer, facing the early morning sun.

Curious as to what he fixed his gaze on, I rose and approached the screen door. The sky spread out above the tree tops, cumulus clouds lazily floating through the unending sea of cornflower blue like tremendous snow white creatures, their shapes ever shifting as they journeyed westward. Not caring that I still wore my nightgown, I opened the screen door and stepped outside.Drawn to the incredible beauty above and awed by the feeling of reverence that filled me, I joined my grandfather in his church.

CHAPTER EIGHT

AUTUMN OF DREAMLESS SLEEP

Beads of cold sweat collected beneath the collar of my cotton sweater and traveled the length of my spine, bringing awareness to each aching vertebrae. Leaning forward, feigning interest in the contents of my purse, I grasped my stomach as another wave of burning nausea reminded me that I should be in the hospital or, at the very least, at home in bed. The discomfort passed and I sat up on the hard wooden gymnasium bleacher, shifting for a more comfortable position. In a ringed mat, Billy Gibson, the one hundred nineteen pound star of the Harris-Lake Park Wolves wrestling team, grappled with his opponent for the title of district champion. I locked my eyes on his sinewy strong body as Billy locked his adversary in a cradle hold, seconds from the slap of the referee's hand on the mat and his tenth consecutive victory. Twisting Billy's class ring again and again on my finger, love and pride shone through the haze clouding my vision and I overrode the blistering acid that churned in my gut. The crowd screamed his name in frenzied anticipation as the cheerleaders, kneeling beside the mat, hollered until their voices grew raspy, their palms rhythmically slapping the floor to the chant.

"Roll him over! Lay him flat! Pin his shoulders to the mat!"

The opposing school's fans roared from across the gym for a reversal, but Billy inched their wrestler's shoulders closer to the floor, the ref laying flat on his belly, hand poised, whistle clenched between his teeth. Billy's mother sprang to her feet, my heart pounded, and the spectators in front of us yelled, "You got him, Gibson!"

Tension surged through the packed bleachers in waves and I struggled to my feet, faltering from the weakness in my limbs. Using the edge of the seat to support my knees, I felt the room spin. The screams, the shouts, and the incessant slap of palms against mat made my temples throb, but I could not shut the noise out. It riddled me from all sides like machine gun fire and, as the referee's hand hit the floor with a crack and Billy shot to his feet, arm thrust high in victory, my legs melted. The echoing applause, the ringing of flesh striking flesh transported my mind from the joyous mayhem of the moment into the recent days of desperation and despondency.

I had landed a solid blow against my father's cheek and he had scrambled to retrieve his glasses from the pavement while fighting to pull my limp body from the car. The emergency room attendant and the nurse hurried forward with a gurney, their loud commands drowning out my moans and incoherent pleas to be left alone.

"Quit flailing or we will have to restrain you. We're going to help. You must cooperate with us."

The attendant wrapped his arms around my chest and hauled me onto the gurney, my head listlessly bobbing like a rag doll, consciousness slowly trickling away. My mother's voice followed fast and frantic through the double doors as rectangles of florescent light passed by the slits of my eyelids and the nurse rushed, her fingers fumbling, to find my pulse.

"She started vomiting last night and she was really listless this morning when I tried to wake her. She says her stomach is burning."

The prick of a needle inserted in my forearm dragged me back from the fog and I blinked at the faces, distorted and dream-like, looming over me. My mother, suspended like a face seen from the other side of a fish bowl, dabbed her muted brown eyes, their edges seeming to blur and fade into the contours of her cheek and I tried to lift my hand to comfort her, but could not.

"Her blood sugar is over eight hundred. She's a coma risk."

The blurry brown eyes darted in the direction of the authoritative voice.

"We're going to start intravenous fluids and an insulin drip, Mrs. Krout. Keep your daughter alert. We don't want her to fall asleep. I'm sending in the technician to get an arterial blood gas"

The authoritative voice departed the examination room, attached to the quick soft thud of rubber soles, leaving my mother to fend off the velvet embrace that beckoned, promising relief. She gripped my arm, shaking it, her fingernails digging into my flesh, until I moaned, forcing my eyes open. But my limbs grew heavy, invisible sandbags pinning them to the bed and my lids sank shut, their weight too much to bear.

"Wake up! Damn it, Amy! Don't go to sleep!" she screamed, slapping my face again and again.

My cheeks tingled with the sting of her blows, but I couldn't resist the pull that drew me deeper and deeper down the long lightless corridor, her wails, strangled sobs, and the crisp crack of her hand against my face growing more distant and faint until only silence and darkness remained.

The brittle brown leaves swirled over the dying lawn beyond the hospital window, children trudging by, on their way to school, bundled tightly in hats and scarves to protect them from the chilly November wind. I slept. The mid-day traffic passed: dusty pick-ups driven by farmers, coming to town for the diner's blue plate special, local gossip at the grain elevator, and to take their wives to beauty parlor appointments. I slept. In the fading autumnal light of afternoon, the bare trees cast long shadows against the brick hospital walls. And still I slept. Hours elapsed and, removed from time's passage and the events traveling on it, I floated in a state of non-existence, my parents, watching and waiting. When the school children, the dusty trucks, and the long shadows returned to their origin and the halogen street lamps flickered in the twilight, I, too, returned.

"Merle, it's almost dinner time. You should get something to eat."

He shook his head and reached to rub her slumped shoulders.

"I'm not hungry. Can I bring you something?"

She took one of his hands from her neck and held it.

"No, I'm not hungry, either."

Their words, muffled and distant, rippled the surface of my dreamless sleep and I strained to grab the auditory lifeline. Another feminine voice, calm and conciliatory, trickled through the silence, the tones closer and more audible than before.

"Any signs of waking up yet? I suspect she'll be coming around soon. The insulin has had a chance to work and we're giving her plenty of fluids to ward off dehydration. Hang tough. Your daughter's going to recover."

Wanting desperately to prove the woman right, I willed my hands to move, but the invisible sandbags were still pressing them against my bare legs. But, slowly, awareness returned to my mind and body and with it, the effects of gastroenteritis and the diabetic keto-acidosis—DKA—that resulted from it. Noticing the slight movement in my fingers, my mother stood, stroked my forehead and said my name. Dad grasped my foot and squeezed it. I opened my eyes to slits, unable to stand the harsh white light, and he flipped the light switch, bathing the room in soothing shadow for my re-entry into the conscious world. My tongue was thick and pasty between parched cracked lips, making it difficult to speak.

"Thirsty," I whispered, trying hard, but not finding any saliva.

My father poured ice water into a plastic cup, the clink of the frozen chips against the rim and the splash of the liquid causing every dehydrated cell in my body to scream with impatience. He held the cup to my lips and I gulped the water, taking the ice chips and holding them against my sticky tongue, but the sweet relief of the drink lasted for only a moment before the liquid hit my stomach. I cried out, the water reacting like lighter fluid on the smoldering embers of my severely irritated stomach lining. The nurse brought a bowl of ice chips, suggesting that I take one at a time. As the burning subsided, the thirst returned and, in desperation, I took one, but as it melted and the small trickles of water hit, the fire roared out of control.

I saw my agony carved in my mother's face, and, with all the strength I could find in my weak grip, I grasped her hand, trying to reassure her, all the while hating the little monster and the damage it had brought our family. For more than a decade, the ugly creature had lurked inside of me, stealing chunks of childhood, leaving only fragmented bits of life as a healthy young girl behind as a cruel and unsatisfying taste of what growing up without its insidious invasion might have been like. Over the years, I had used an assortment of strategies to battle the monster. On its arrival, I believed its power would diminish in the light and I openly spoke of it to all the adults and children around me. Later, I believed its power would diminish if it was not unique and I spent the summer at a camp with other kids who carried their own monsters.

As I became a teenager, I believed its power would diminish through denial, rarely speaking of it and hiding the signs of its existence from as many people as possible. For those who already knew, I played down the situation, crediting it only as a minor detail. This method seemed to be agreeable to the monster, as it quietly festered, surprisingly forgiving of the bad diabetic habits to which I had grown comfortable. I indulged in desserts. I drank beer at keg parties. I smoked cigarettes. I thought I had found a loophole and that I was the exception to the rules that dictate diabetic health. With a sense of invincibility only teens seem to have, I ran like a foolish dog who forgets about the collar around her neck, so sure I had won my freedom from the beast by ignoring it, not once looking over my shoulder to see it smiling and gripping an uncoiling leash in its mean little fist. As the flames licked the walls of my belly and the lines deepened in my mother's face, the pain resonated like evil laughter in my head, jerking me back towards the truth.

"Stupid girl! Did you think you were free? You are a diabetic. You will always be a diabetic. I am yours and you are mine. Forever. Don't fight it. You can't win!"

I left the hospital a day later, with the sobering reality that I might not win the fight I had waged against my illness pushed to the rear of my thoughts. With obstinate pride at the forefront, I set out to dance around the ring for a few more rounds, hoping to survive the punches thrown at me.

Although my stomach hadn't healed yet and my mother argued against it, I was determined to go to the wrestling invitational to see Billy compete.

"Don't you think you should stay home and rest?" my mother said on the way home. "Billy will understand that you aren't in good enough shape to go to his wrestling match. I'm sure he knows what a serious thing a diabetic coma is. He can come over and visit you after he gets home from the meet."

I panicked, mortified by the idea of my boyfriend knowing what had happened.

"No, Billy can't know about the coma. Please don't say anything about it to him. Please, Mom, I don't want anyone to know. He'll think I'm a freak. Everyone will think I'm a sick diabetic freak!

"He knows you were in the hospital, Amy. You missed school. What are you planning on telling him?"

"I'll tell him I had the flu. That's all it really was, anyway. Just a really bad flu. I feel a lot better already. I'm sure by this afternoon, I'll be fine," I said, my aching belly calling me a liar."Can I please go?"

Mom shifted in the passenger's seat, turning her attention towards my dad.

"What do you think, Merle? Should she go?"

He paused for a long moment before answering. I glanced at his profile from the back seat and recognized his expression as one from another autumn day so many years ago when he was told that I had diabetes. He watched a herd of cattle clustered together at the corner of a weedy paddock, their heads bowed, vapor clouding from their nostrils as they waited for the gray sky to snow, his eyes filled with sadness and guilt. He lived with his own little monster and he knew the power it could wield, for it had, in previous years, temporarily blinded him and taken part of his foot. During my parents' engagement, he, too, had fallen into the deep dreamless sleep, brought to the brink of death by shingles and a subsequent staph infection. His recovery had been long and arduous, but when the ordeal was done, he married my mother with a new-found sense of respect for, and trepidation of, life. She was eager to start a family, but he resisted, afraid that he again would fall ill and be unable to care for a wife and children. There also was the risk that his offspring could be genetically predisposed to diabetes, a fate he did not wish for them. But my mother, being very young and hopeful, lovingly convinced him that life should not be stifled by "what ifs," and I, born during the early autumn blizzard of 1969, had arrived breech, but healthy and whole. For the first five years, my father grew more grateful with each day that passed and I flourished, untouched by the monster's claws, and he began to release himself from the foreboding of the future that had gripped him before my birth. But, as it so often does, the ugly creature that lived inside him waited in silence, feeling my father's relief and knowing it soon would end as it watched its own hideous progeny springing to life inside me.

"This wrestling match," he said, looking in the rear view mirror, "it's pretty important, isn't it?"

"Yes, it is. If Billy wins today, he's only two tournaments away from qualifying for state competition. I can't miss it," I said.

"That kid's a good athlete. I saw him play football earlier this year. He made some nice catches." The comment threw me a little. My dad hadn't ever been much of a conversationalist when it came to my relationship with Billy. The topic of love and sex and romance were "girl talk" and considered my Mom's turf. Dad's attention towards the young man dating his only daughter had been limited to icy greetings and suspicious glances. Proud that my boyfriend's talent had been acknowledged, I leaned towards the front seat, grinning at my dad.

"Yeah, he's a starting running back, but I think he might try the quarterback position next year, if the coach will let him."

Dad nodded, but didn't appear too impressed."How are you going to get to the meet?"

"Billy's parents invited me to go with them."

"Are you really feeling better?"

He held my gaze in the mirror for a moment, seeing the truth, waiting to hear another lie.

"Yeah, I'm feeling better."

"Well, you know how you feel. If you think you're all right and your blood sugar is where it should be, I don't see why not."

"Thanks, Dad"

He couldn't retrieve the stolen moments of my childhood, the slumber parties from which I had been excluded, the after-school games of tag I had been too tired to play, or the Halloween I finally gave up on trick or treating, embittered by the bag of candy that I could not eat. But at that moment, he gave me what I, like most teen girls, wanted the most: the opportunity to be normal. For as we rode along the highway, away from the Osceola County Hospital, we drove away from the recollections of doctors, disease, and diabetic comas. And, as the miles faded behind us, I was no longer the fragile unconscious victim, but just another girl on her way to a wrestling meet.

***

The crowd thinned in the gymnasium, the final match over, and Billy emerged from the locker room, his duffle bag slung over one shoulder. Grinning, he slid his arm around my waist and handed me the gold medal.

"Nice job," I said, holding the medallion and beaming with pride despite persistent aches and stings.

"I missed you down on the mat. I don't think the cheerleaders yell as loud without their captain."

He pulled me closer and the pressure against my body made me wince.

"That flu was really bad. But I'll cheer next week."

"How are you feeling? Are you going to be up for Joe's party tonight? His parents are out of town this weekend. It should be pretty wild."

Two girls passed, giggling and smiling.

"Great match, Billy. We'll see you at Joe's later, right?" the pretty blond said, tossing her hair and winking at him.

Billy's head turned, his handsome brown eyes sparkling at the blonde's flirtation. The acid churn in my stomach and I shot a look in her direction. She shot back, but I narrowed my eyes, my tone icy.

"We'll both be there," I said.

"I'll catch you later then, Billy," she cooed, all teased hair and white teeth and big breasts. Not wanting him to see the wave of emotion that suddenly threatened to break my illusion of confidence, I pulled away from him, muttering that I needed to find the restroom.

"Sure, I'll meet you out front," he said, still watching the blond.

Moving through the exiting spectators, I fought to keep composure, my teeth clenched on my throbbing lip, until I reached the ladies room, where, alone in a stall, I buried my face in my jacket and sobbed. It was not just the ache of my belly or the pretty girl's overtures towards Billy that caused the tears of bitterness; it was anxiety and regret. The cloak of denial I had protected myself with for so long was unraveling and I deeply regretted having ever chosen to hide beneath it.

For as it disappeared and my peers, including Billy, saw what was beneath it, they would certainly turn away, unable to deal with the raw truth about the cheerleader, the senior class officer, the yearbook editor they had come to know. The statute of limitations on my erroneous act was nearing its expiration and soon the crepe paper streamers, the pink roses of a prom corsage, and the yearbook photographs would fade and crumble and I, stripped of my "All-American Girl" costume, would face the reality of my true identity. I looked down at the heart-shaped pendant dangling on its fine chain, the kind of birthday gift a million other teenage boys had given a million other teenage girls.

"Do you like it?" Billy had asked as we snuggled in the back seat of his car and I opened the little crush velvet box.

Freeing the delicate chain, I had held it and considered the perfectly shaped gold heart. It reflected nothing of my truer self and I loved it. He had kissed me, full and deep, all the electric tingles and heated sexual tension of first love crackling between us.

"It's like you," I had said."Perfect."

I washed my face without looking into the mirror and left the restroom. Only the red illuminated letters of an exit sign glowed in the corridor. As my eyes adjusted, I noticed the large mural that adorned the wall above the row of lockers. Cartoon caricatures depicting school mascots of the Cornbelt Conference were painted in bright glossy colors across the cinder blocks, and I recognized the royal blue and white wolf that represented our high school. The foolish looking figure with bulging eyes and droopy ears appeared more Looney Tunes than lupine, more absurdity than animal. I walked beside the line of lockers, until one image in particular caused me to stop and stare, my chest tightening, shoulders tensing.

From the cinder block, an Indian stared back with a face no less foolish than the wolf and I blinked, unable to detach myself from it or the way it chilled the blood in my veins. He squatted on stunted legs, a brown loin cloth and moccasins his only clothing, his tiny fist gripping a war club as if prepared to leap and strike a blow. His head and body were mismatched, the face monstrous atop the miniature arms legs, and chest, like some kind of fierce boy-man. But it was his eyes that were the most alarming. They protruded like two black peas, devoid of intelligence and emotion, the artist's rendering giving birth to something less than human. My father's blood rushed quick and hot, and my heart beat behind my ribs like a caged bird. The red light of the exit marker fell across my cheeks and the cartoon Indian grinned, scarlet slashes decorating his cheeks, too.

"Are you lost?"

Startled, I jerked my head towards the gray-haired man standing at the opposite end of the hallway with a push broom leaned against a stooped shoulder. Without answering, I bolted, leaving my twentieth-century war paint glowing on the floor behind me. I ran the length of the empty corridor until I reached the double glass doors. Thrusting them open, I plunged into the frigid night air. My lungs stung and rage fanned the fire in my blood, its blistering heat burning hotter than the fire in my scorched belly.

CHAPTER NINE

WINTER OF THE LONE TREE

The gravel road wound, pale and empty, through the rural landscape of lush black fields, the freshly plowed soil unfolding beside it like the luxurious fabric of a supple ebony blanket. I drove fast, clouds of dust rising behind the car until the trees that bordered Silver Lake came into view and I slowed, knowing I was almost there. Another quarter mile and I released my white-knuckled grip from the steering wheel and exhaled, seeing it off to the right in the distance, tall and stark standing at the fence line of a barren pasture, the lone tree.

It wasn't the first time that I had been drawn to this place, feeling a kindred connection to the tree, nor was I the only one who felt the strange bond to it. J.D., a drummer and Jim Morrison disciple and one of my few male confidants, was attracted to the tree, as well. He had often driven his old pickup truck to the west end of the lake just to look at the dark skeletal trunk and bare branches reaching from the earth like the spirit of what the land once had been, ripping through the fabric of time. Our shared love of photography had habitually led my friend, Nora, and I to the hill beneath the ancient tree.

"It makes you think of loneliness. Doesn't it?" she had said, as she focused her camera lens on the solitary scene.

It did make me think of loneliness. It was loneliness that often brought me to the isolated tree and it was loneliness that brought me there now. Pulling off into the empty gravel parking area beside the lake, I turned off the engine and sat staring through the dusty windshield at the sentinel on the hill, my heart aching. Gusts of wind blew west off the choppy water, breaking whitecaps against the shore and rustling the leaves of the maples, cottonwoods, and elms that skirted the lake. The tree on the hill remained silent and still, untouched by the force of the changing June gale. I admired its strength.

Stepping from the car, I walked to the cement boat ramp and squinted across the rough green water to the opposite shore where the town met the lake and where my father now sat, alone in a house that no longer seemed like a home to either one of us. Thin gray clouds hung like wisps of smoke on the eastern skyline and my thoughts drifted to unwanted destinations.

It had been the smell of smoke that halted me at the back door, apprehension creeping over me, when I returned from school. The usual aroma of dinner cooking on the stove was absent and, although most of the lights were on, an eerie quiet filled the rooms. I hesitated at the entrance to the kitchen, startled to find my mother seated at the table, a lit cigarette in her hand.

"Why are you smoking?"

I hadn't seen her take so much as a drag since she had quit ten years earlier. Ignoring the question, she laid the cigarette in an ashtray, which had accumulated several crumpled butts, and spoke in a soft shaky voice.

"I'm sorry, Amy. I never meant to hurt you or your dad. It just happened."

"What just happened?"

I've fallen in love with someone else. I'm leaving."

The impact of the words jolted me like a speeding car suddenly thrown in reverse as the meaning of what she said rooted in my brain. The contents of my mind toppled upside down into a jumbled pile, confession and confusion entangling with the images of her cigarettes and packed suitcases. Memories of my friends' insinuations about her and the man she had claimed as "just an old friend" and my defense of her actions, while all the time believing the alibis and denials she had given me, surfaced and my disbelief quickly turned to anger.

She rose from her chair, moving closer to comfort me, but the cold bitterness in my voice caused her to shrink back as though she had been slapped.

"You lied to me," I hissed through clenched teeth."You lied to Dad. You lied to everybody."

The whistle blew from atop the city water tower, indicating that it was six o'clock. And I looked at the table where, on any other night, our family would have been eating dinner. Dad would have been recounting his dealings with demanding customers at the Chevrolet dealership, Mom would have been dishing up meatloaf and green beans, and I would have been waiting for the right moment to ask permission to go to the movies with Billy on Friday. But, on this night, there were no dinner plates on the table, only a filthy ashtray. The chair my father usually sat in was empty and a cardboard box filled with books and papers sat on mine.

"I really didn't mean to hurt anyone. I love you. Please try to understand. I can't stay here. I have to leave."

"Is he going to run out on his family, too? Is that the plan? I suppose the two of you have it figured out."

"He's telling his kids and their mother tonight. We want to be together. This is the only way."

"Where are you going to live?"

"I'm going to stay with Grandpa and Grandma for a while."

"Is he going to stay there, too? Are Grandpa and Grandma going to let him in their house?"

"I don't know, but I'll be there until we can find someplace to live."

My stomach churned at the thought of them sleeping at my grandparent's house together, wanting Grandma and Grandpa to be as angry at my mother as I was and to hate the man who had betrayed my father as much as I did.

"Does Dad know any of this?"

"I haven't told him yet. I'm waiting for him. He had to work late."

"Well, I'm not sticking around for this bullshit. I've heard all I can take. I hope you have a wonderful life," I spat, swallowing back the urge to cry and hurling the book bag I still held onto the linoleum.

I zipped my ski jacket and fished in the pocket of my jeans for car keys as she rose again to grab my sleeve. Violently, I tore my arm free and glared at her anguished expression.

"Don't touch me! You made your choice. You chose him. You didn't choose Dad and you didn't choose me. You chose him!"

"It's not a choice between him and you, Amy. I love you and I always will. Loving him doesn't change that. I'm your mother. I love you. Please don't ever forget that. I'm your mother and I love you!" she pleaded as I pulled my boots on at the back door.

"That's not how I see it."

I slammed the door, the glass rattling in the porch window as if it might shatter in my wake. I didn't look back as I gunned the engine of the old Vega and skidded out of the driveway, snow, ice, and gravel flying from the tires.

Lake Park's two-block business district was quiet, most of the shopkeepers having gone home for the night. The faint glow of a Pepsi sign illuminated the dark interior of Butch's City Market and the pharmacist stood in front of the drug store, exhaling visible breaths into the frigid air as he locked up. He smiled and waved a gloved hand as I sped down the hill past Chuck's Tavern and the Silver Lanes Bowling Alley, where three pickup trucks and a rusted Buick sat parked for the evening, the vehicles' owners comfortably perched on their regular stools at the bar.

My uncle, John, filled his car with gas outside of the station beside the feed store and he waved, but, like the pharmacist's greeting, I ignored him, staring straight out the frosty windshield, fixed on an unknown point of destination. Driving ten miles over the speed limit, I pushed the accelerator down, headed towards Highway 9, not caring that the roads were much too icy for such recklessness. When I reached the intersection for the highway, the Vega slid, fishtailing towards the ditch then swerving back towards the stop sign, my heart pounding wildly. Unable to bring the car to a stop, I spun it onto the deserted highway without stopping and slammed down the accelerator again.

The lanes were clear of snow and I relaxed my grip on the wheel, rummaging for my own secret stash of cigarettes hidden under the driver's seat, thinking that my mother was not the only one who needed a vice to fall back on this night. Lighting a Marlboro, I inhaled deeply, savoring the slight burn in my chest and the soothing rush in my head as the smoke invaded my lungs and the chemicals hit my brain. Not knowing where I was going and not caring, as long as the road took me away from the smoky kitchen, the packed suitcases, and the desperate wounded look I had left in my mother's eyes, I drove west along the empty black top until I reached the intersecting gravel road that led to the lakeshore and the lone tree.

Without realizing it, I braked and turned onto the ice-packed gravel. It did not seem to be a conscious decision, but a call that my heart, not my head, was answering, and, never before having felt such a yearning to see the ancient tree, I surrendered to it. But as I clicked the headlights brighter in the thick blackness, I discovered drifts of snow crisscrossing the road, making it impassable to a vehicle without four-wheel drive. I stopped the car and leaned forward, straining to see the lone tree in the darkness. I knew that it was too far from where I had been forced to stop to see it. Finally, accepting that the efforts were futile, I shut off the car, turned off the headlights and slouched back against the seat, defeated, drained, and distanced from everyone and everything in which I had once found comfort.

The darkness, the silence, and the winter chill encircled me in my solitude like a cocoon and I let the tears trickle their warmth down my cold cheeks and chin. Why did stability and security never seem to last very long? Why the plateau you were standing on did just seconds before erode under your feet, sending you plummeting towards the unknown? How was it possible that I was a happy carefree teenage girl, attending cheerleading practice at five o'clock and, at six o'clock, the enraged daughter of a dysfunctional family whose wife and mother was running off with the neighbor man? The questions raced through my head, no answers following, until the absurdity of life sent me into a manic burst of laughter, breaking the silence of the car's interior. I slammed my fists against the steering wheel, the insane combination of sobs and laughter erupting from me in pathetic waves. The pieces that had once fused, regardless how loosely, to create my view of the world had been flung in all directions like a broken jigsaw puzzle, and even if I were able to gather the scattered bits and assemble the picture, it would never again look the same. Too many pieces were lost: my mother, my family, my trust.

The clouds shifted and a sliver of moon shone its opalescent light over the stark white countryside, revealing the old tree as a black silhouette, isolated and monolithic. It stood at the edge of the frozen field where it had, for hundreds of years, survived the force of the prairie winds, the bitter plains' winters, and the axes of generations who had chosen to subdue the land rather than live in harmony with it. Unclenching my fists, I wiped my eyes and focused my attention on my sole reason for sitting, alone and shivering, on the deserted snowy road. I thought of the changes that had come to the tree over the years: the pile of stones that had appeared at its base when the man who owned the pasture in which it stood removed them from his bean field and deposited them out of reach of plow blades; the families of birds and squirrels that had lived among its branches for a season or two before moving on; the scarcity of leaves that budded each new spring as the ancient one grew older. It survived the changes and changed to survive and I, humbled by a kind of honesty and truth that only one who is not human can possess, knew that I, too, must live by this lesson.

Half a year had passed since the night my mother left. I squatted at the edge of the breaking waves, and watched the water's motion send the floating algae on top to the bottom and churn the contents of the bottom to the surface in a continuous cyclical pattern, but I could not find meaning in it all. I had tried to grasp the idea of my mother's happiness as justification for her actions, but that only led me to question the source of her unhappiness. I couldn't face the possibilities with out tapping the darkest center of my own suspicions.

The disquieting, yet plausible, reason for her seeking contentment apart from my father and me had first crept into my mind upon returning home the evening of her departure. The house, which an hour earlier had light shining from every window, sat dark, except for the soft glow of the television in the living room. I found my father there, as he stared, but did not see, the thirty-second shots of smiling actors attaining illusory joy through diet cola, B8 engines, and two pizzas for the price of one as they flashed across the screen. We embraced and I told him that I already knew. I had never seen my father cry, not when he was struggling to retain his eye sight, not when his toe and part of his foot became gangrenous and had to be amputated, not even when the doctor had diagnosed his only child with diabetes, but as we stood holding each other in the semi-darkness, his chest heaved and he sobbed against my shoulder. His tears were gasoline to the rage that burned just below the surface and I was flooded with hatred for my mother and the man she had chosen over Dad. Diabetes had suffocated, scarred, and destroyed parts of his body without him ever shedding a tear, but their betrayal had wounded him in ways disease did not have the power to. They had damaged his pride and his dignity, and the strong handsome man with the dark straight hair and deep brown eyes that I remembered so fondly from childhood, leaned, weeping, against me, his fragility and the brittleness of his condition brutally apparent.

It was in this moment that the insidious explanation for my mother's decision leaked into my thoughts as a possibility. I tried to deny it as a valid reason, thinking it far too cruel and self-absorbed after the many years she had remained with my father, but the idea would not die, the questions pricking my conscious like dozens of dull needles. Had my mother grown dissatisfied after struggling alongside my father as his health declined? Did she feel that she had wasted the best years of her life nursing a chronically ill husband? Where did I fit into her discontent?

Did she want a healthier husband? Did she want healthier children? Had she finally fled to escape the illness from which my father and I could not run?

***

The heat of the June sun caressed my shoulders and the cool green lake water splashed over my toes, cleansing my head of the memories stained with tears and darkness. I removed my sandals and waded into the rolling waves, letting them crash against my calves and knees, relishing the peace that washed through me as I stood firm among the ever-changing movements of the waters. I breathed the pungent smell of the roiled lake, and the subtle scent of sweet grass that arrived unexpectedly on the west wind. Turning, I again saw the lone tree on the hill, its thin growth of new leaves fluttering, and I whispered in silent gratitude to my old friend. It had changed. I had changed. We would survive.

CHAPTER TEN

SPRING OF DISAPPEARING STARS

I woke, after ten hours of sleep, exhausted and confused. Afternoon sunlight flooded the bedroom and I groped for the cord to shut the drapes. The brightness stung my swollen eyes. I glanced at the alarm clock, swore, and dropped back on to the pillow. It was three thirty. I had slept through all four of my classes, even a scheduled literature midterm exam. I fucked up again, I thought, turning my back on the harsh reality of the clock. Like an enemy army, a million morose thoughts prepared for another invasion, and I rubbed my throbbing forehead and temples, waiting for my defense: a recently acquired dose of apathy. It would anesthetize my conscience before the onslaught of shame and self-loathing could set in. Another abbreviated day in a life that lost meaning and direction with each passing hour had begun.

Discarded clothing, open textbooks, and empty beer cans lay in piles on the floor and my foot grazed the pair of bifocals hidden in the mess as I swung my legs out of bed and dragged a wrinkled flannel shirt from the heap. Although the heavy curtains blocked most of the daylight from the room, my eyes still burned and I struggled to focus. I rifled through the books and papers, relocating the glasses that once had only been necessary for reading, but now, after changing to a stronger lens prescription, were always kept within reach. Tucking the snarled hair behind my ears, I slid the glasses on, hoping to alleviate the fuzzy edges of the shadowy room, but they did little to offer the desired clarity.

I stood, groaning from the aches of years not yet lived. Discomfort permeating my body, I shuffled like an old woman into the hallway. The apartment was empty and silent, and, relieved by my roommate's absence, I locked myself in the bathroom. Flipping the light on above the sink, I caught sight of my reflection in the mirror. Tangled strands of hair, dull and limp, framed a pale, puffy face. An eruption of red blemishes along the jaw and the dark circles that tinged the bags beneath my watery, dilated stare were the only traces of color in my otherwise pasty complexion. Disgusted, I threw open the medicine cabinet, preferring the view of prescription bottles, toothpaste, and Band-Aids. I swallowed two aspirin and brushed my teeth, leaving the cabinet door open, the mirror's unwelcome visual truths directed safely towards the shower curtain. As I clicked the cabinet shut and left the bathroom, I stole another furtive glance in the door's surface, hoping to discover some small aspect that I had missed, some tiny feature to remind me of the girl I had been three years earlier, the girl whose discomfort had once been hidden behind a careful smile. But forcing myself to assess the reflection again only emphasized the transformation I had undergone since my parents' divorce, since leaving home, since Grandpa Jack's death. The girl was gone and in her place, a woman with tired lonely eyes and a cynical scowl looked back at me, the dark contents of her heart revealed in every furrow, every wrinkle, every line.

The persistent weight of fatigue threatened to pull me back to the comfort of the rumpled bed, but I resisted, selecting a thick psychology text from the pile on the floor and heading to the kitchen for some strong coffee. The Iowa River ran quick and clear, the last remnants of melting ice riding on its currents and I watched the university students feeding the flocks of excited ducks that gathered on the banks near the foot bridge. I opened the window and inhaled the pleasing mixture of fresh spring air still tinged with the crisp chill of winter. In the distance, the toll of the Old Capital's bell sounded from beneath the golden dome high above the Pent crest. The crab apple branches, once dark and dormant under the spell of winter, now wore thousands of budding leaves, the tree's boughs appearing enveloped by a cloud of vibrant green energy. My thoughts turned to the bouquets of pink crab apple blossoms I, as a small child, had picked for my mother each April. Hope and anticipation lifted my spirits as the flower's sweet scent drifted through my memory. But the trees outside the window wouldn't bloom for several weeks and a gust of chilly wind blew off of the river, causing me to shiver, reminding me of an unpleasant possibility. A late snowfall could tear the new petals from their branches, leaving the tree barren of fruit until next year. Spring made no promises to fragile flowers.

I shut the kitchen window and carried the book and coffee mug to a well-lit corner of the living room. I settled onto the threadbare sofa, sipping from the cup while adjusting my bifocals. Preparing to tackle the task I had failed to complete the previous night, I set the coffee down and exhaled. I turned to a chapter on cognitive learning and leaned closer to the page, squinting at the small print. After four paragraphs, it became apparent that the problems that had forced me to throw the text to the floor the night before weren't resolved. Words blurred, running into one another and disappearing, leaving blank white space where letters and punctuation should have been. I plowed on, the terror of failure biting at my heels. Concentrating on each sentence, I willed the words to appear, and when they didn't, I begged. I pulled the page closer to my face and tilted it forward, causing some of the missing characters to take shape.

Their reappearance encouraged me and I proceeded, continuously moving the cumbersome text. I blinked my eyes and shifted the book to every possible angle until the end of one agonizing chapter was in sight. But before I could finish, a sharp burning sensation stabbed at the backs of my eyes like a hot knife and the remaining words swirled out of focus.

"What's wrong with these fucking glasses?" I screamed.

Bolting from the couch, I abandoned the open book and retreated to my room where I hurled the offending bifocals at the bed. I threw myself on the mattress beside them and dug in the drawer of the nightstand. The baggie was tucked at the rear and I yanked it out, eager to seek relief in its contents. I rolled a joint and lit it. Taking a hit, I laid staring at the ceiling, waiting for the smoke to float my mind from its misery. But my irritation only melted into melancholy and I ended up on the floor with a photo album in my lap.

The pictures, changed by the knowledge that time unveils, no longer simply existed as captive fragments of memory behind the protection of yellowing plastic. All the meaning and the emotion that had been missed in the moment glared like bare white bones. All the things that, in the past, had been so easy to deny or to overlook, screamed for acknowledgement. The faces with guarded eyes and transparent smiles covered the album's pages like a prologue of images to the sad chapters of my family's story. The Christmas snapshot of Grandpa Jack hinted of the undiagnosed cancer festering in his lungs; his cheeks hollow, his skin sallow, I posed, sitting on his lap, with my hair plated in two long braids and clutching a doll for which I was much too old.

"I miss you," I said to the old man, the girl, and the doll.

I turned the pages and saw my mother's forced smile as she stood beside my father, drifts of snow their backdrop. A wool dress coat hid her figure, but her weight was apparent in the fullness of her face. She wore no lipstick. He wore no gloves. They didn't touch.

I squinted at the New Year's Eve photo, recognizing the longing and dissatisfaction in my mother's face. It was an expression I had seen in the mirror earlier. Suddenly aware of my own physical decline, I unbuttoned the flannel shirt and rubbed the roll of fat. Too much beer and pizza delivery had turned my flat abdomen into a ring of flab. I hatefully pinched it until a bruise tattooed my skin.

Flipping the pages, I glimpsed the shot of Billy and me dancing beneath a canopy of balloons and crepe paper. The beads and sequins of my gown shimmered and his brown eyes sparkled. He had whispered in my ear that he loved me as we swayed in each other's arms, the memory of my parents' recent divorce magically barred from the moment.

"Forever?" I had asked.

"Forever," he had promised.

But "forever" ended a month later and the souvenir prom picture only dredged up buried feelings of bitterness and abandonment

The last three pictures were loose and I pulled back the plastic, adhering them to the sticky cardboard. At the top of the page, I placed the five by seven of my father and his new wife, Sandy. They stood at the altar of a church, his arm around her waist, her head resting against his shoulder. I positioned the horizontal shot of my mother holding hands with the man for whom she had left my father, the man who was now her husband, beneath it. I considered his kind blue eyes and his warm smile peeking through his graying beard. Dennis was not a bad man. His love for her was evident, as was her happiness. But shifting my gaze from my mother's girlish grin to my father's proud smile, I could not share their joy or their contentment. Where did I fit in their new marriages, their new families, their new lives? Perhaps adult children of divorce were not meant to "fit" in their parents' redesigned futures. Again, I stared at the two happy couples and I ached with envy, knowing that a broken family was not the sole source of my loneliness. I wanted the love, the acceptance, the fulfillment that they had found in their relationships, but, with the ugliness in my heart far surpassing the ugliness in the mirror, I did not believe myself worthy.

Holding the last snapshot close to my weary eyes, I examined its details before arranging it in the album. Great Grandmother Tott sat, surrounded by grandchildren, a decorated sheet cake on the picnic table in front of her. "Happy 85th Birthday" adorned the white frosting in pink icing letters. As I smoothed the plastic sheet over the pictures, a peculiar remembrance of the celebration crept into my thoughts.

Staring up at the cloudless night sky, Grandma Tott had narrowed her eyes and frowned, taking her thick glasses off and wiping them on the hem of her sweater.

"There just aren't as many stars as when I was a girl," she had said.

I shut the book of photographs and slid it under the bed, my thoughts lingering on her words, words that had not revealed their hidden meaning until now. I thought of the dozens of blank white pages remaining in the album, wondering what images, if any, would fill the emptiness. I thought of the Polaroid pictures shoved deep in the pigeonhole of my desk. But they did not belong in the family album, their content too gruesome, too honest. The "Eye Care Associates" envelope containing them had been hidden behind a box of paper clips for six months and I had not seen the pictures since the optometrist had interpreted their meaning. But the hidden photos would not be ignored, unleashing their dreaded message from beyond the dark crevice of the desk. They transformed themselves from squares of glossy paper into nightmarish dreams of drowning that plagued my sleep. They solidified into the immense invisible stone that lay in the pit of my chest. They liquefied into the corrosive acid that ate holes in my stomach. Escape was impossible.

I clicked on the lamp and slouched onto the desk chair. The pigeonhole loomed like a dark and dangerous corridor leading to the chamber where my greatest uncertainties lurked. I plunged my hand into the recess. The pointed corner of the paper clip box jabbed my wrist and I snatched the envelope from the cubby, jerking my hand out as if bitten by something poisonous. Unsealing it, I withdrew the pictures. The optometrist had jotted in the white space at the bottom in blue ink and I picked up the one marked "Right". The pink plain of retinal tissue was covered with red vessels like blood rivers, their tributaries, thin and spidery, extending in all directions.

"These aren't healthy vessels. It's fairly common in diabetic patients, problems with circulation. They'll eventually need treatment to prevent vision loss," the optometrist had said, handing the pictures to me and writing the name of a retinal specialist on a business card.

I fished the card from the envelope. It was time to make the phone call. But the name and number was blurry and unreadable. I tucked the card, along with the pictures, back into the envelope. Clicking off the lamp, I sat in the shadows, unable to move, unable to think, unable to cry. Mind disconnected from body. Body disconnected from spirit. Spirit disconnected from mind. In the void, the monster's voice came, rising as a whisper out of the darkest and most dank caverns of my soul.

"Your mother left. Billy left. Your grandfather left. But I will never leave. Ever."

Rage bubbled, oily and black, into my brain and my hands balled into fists.

"I hate you," I hissed between clenched teeth, "I hate you! I hate you! I hate you!"

I seized the envelope and tore it and its contents to shreds. Knocking the chair to the floor, I grabbed the bifocals from the bed and threw them against the wall.

"I hate you!"

I attacked the bed pillow, brutally beating it with my fists until the muscles of my arm strained. The fury consumed me and I fell to the floor, clutching the pillow to my face, muffling my screams. When my rage was spent, I lay, fetal, on the dirty carpet. Hours passed. I remained limp among the tattered pieces of photograph. The rigid spine of a philosophy text pressed against my bare foot. I kicked it, taunted by its disappearing words. As I stared through the window's smudged glass, the last sliver of daylight vanished from the horizon and the disappearing stars dotted the night.

CHAPTER ELEVEN

AUTUMN OF
THE LAUGHING JESUS

A dry brown leaf made its slow swirling descent from a tree's bare branch and I stared at it through the psychologist's office window. Watching it fall until it sank from view below the bottom slat of the Venetian blinds, I wondered if it was a leaf at all. It might have been a bird or a discarded paper bag. Failing vision only provided possibilities, never certainties. Aggravated, I leaned across the arm of the chair and lifted the corner of the dusty slats, focused on identifying the falling object. But, from the second floor window, I only saw the frozen ground beneath a naked tree shift with shades of brown motion. I dropped the slat, pressure building behind my eyes.

Dr. Dee Davison scribbled something on the yellow legal pad, laid her pen down, and swiveled in the desk chair. Resting her elbows against her knees, she formed a steeple with her index fingers and propped her prominent chin on it.

"Why did you try to commit suicide?"

The skin of my wrists tingled and I clutched my arm, pressing a thumb hard against the spot. I resented the soft scarless flesh, the vein's defiant throbbing, and the therapist's desire to shine an analytical searchlight into my darkest corners. Dr. Davison waited, her serious face still balanced on the two fine-boned fingers. She appeared immune to the oppressive weight of the silence that filled the space between us, the same silence that slumped my shoulders and kept my eyes pinned to the scuffed toes of my boots. Biting at a chapped lip, I looked up and chose the framed picture to the left of her cropped blond head, my one good eye dodging the psychologist's probing glance. The charcoal lines lay trapped under glass, beige mat and metal frame, their meaning as elusive as my answer to the question.

"Tell me about that night," she said, unfolding her hands and leaning back in the chair."What were you thinking? What were you feeling?"

I squeezed my wrist tighter as the tingling increased and the blood pulsed beneath the brutal grip of my fingernails.

Loneliness had held me fast in its brutal grip and the silent midnight hour had descended, draping everything in its unbearable darkness. Pain pounded like a war drum behind the gauze eye patch, and the lumpy sofa bed dug into my spine. Groping for the codeine on the end table, I found the prescription bottle empty and threw it aside. A water glass toppled, a pile of magazines sliding to the floor with it. In the apartment's only bedroom, my mother stirred, startled by the commotion.

"Are you all right?" she called, the words slurred by sleep, tinged with alarm.

I had held my breath and silently pleaded for her to return to sleep, torn between the need to cry out for maternal comfort and my concern at needing it too much. Mom didn't deserve the infliction of my misery, not again, after so many other hours, so many other nights, so many years. She couldn't soothe me any longer. The narcotics didn't even relieve it. Nothing took it away anymore.

When she finally retreated into sleep, exhaustion winning one of the many battles it waged against her, the hushed sound of her snoring taunted me in the darkness and whispered of the sweet release for which I yearned. Scratching at the cloth tape around the patch, I fought the urge to dig my fingers into the wounded eye as the surgical incisions began to sting and itch again, a spear driving into my temple and vanquishing any hope of sleep. I whimpered, balling the offending hand into a fist and biting the knuckle. My will relinquished to the woes of my body and mind, and I drifted from the moment into memory and back again, a tortured soul imprisoned in an anguished shell. Resentment, bitterness, and hatred clung to my conscious like the musty layers of a shroud, and the jagged edged reality that fellow mourners for the loss of my eyesight were few and far betweencut deeper and more destructively than the surgeon's scalpel ever could. The names of those who no longer called or came to visit echoed in the void along with their indirect greetings, their clumsy excuses, their empty promises.

"Say hello to Amy. Tell her I hope she's feeling better," they said with a half-smile, hurrying down the street before my mother could mention how easy it would be for them to deliver the message themselves or how much more it would mean conveyed in person.

"No, I didn't know you had another eye surgery. That's really rough. Well … I should probably get going. I'm pretty busy," they said on the rare occasion I reached them by phone, hoping for some conversation, some companionship, some consolation.

"It was good to … uh … see you. We should get together soon. Maybe after the holidays, when things settle down at work. Maybe when your … situation … well, take care," they said, disconcerted by my dilated pupil, my eye patch, my unexpected presence as I walked on my father's arm through the mall.

Life had been reduced to an endless ebb and flow of physical ache and intense isolation, one only receding long enough for the other to drown me in its darkness and despair. I had lost all connection to people, places, pleasure; my suitcase packed, never knowing from day to day whether I would return to the hospital or to my grandparent's or to the one bedroom apartment my mother and Dennis shared. Their tender care and kindness couldn't erase the feelings I dragged from house to house along with the battered luggage, the feeling I had become a burden to my family, a uselessand cumbersome weight around the necks of those whom I loved and who loved me. It would only get worse. Blindness was imminent and would force my dependence on them. No matter how great the responsibility, they, out of love, would accept the role of full-time caregiver without complaint.

The muffled sounds of mixers and sliding metal pans floated through the floor boards as the old man and his helpers started their graveyard shift in the bakery below; bed springs creaked as my mother rolled in her sleep. In the kitchen, a clock ticked, keeping time with the slow steady beat that pulsed behind my eye patch. I listened, my ears straining to hear the sounds of the living, the mundane sounds that I thought would save me from madness. The rest of my body numbed, the hellish ache of my ravaged eye the only remaining sensation, the tick of the clock the only remaining sound, I lay like a corpse until, in the deep blue minutes just before dawn, the vision came.

It danced on the backs of my eyelids, macabre, yet comforting in its clarity: a stark white room, nooses knotted to rough wooden ceiling beams, the cold bare feet of the dangling dead.

I saw myself, naked, my hands reaching for them like a child grasping for the string of a helium balloon, seeking to join their ascent. As the image melted, its promise of release pulled me from bed, through the shadowy kitchen to the white tile bathroom. I closed the door, turned on the light, and stared, without recognition, at the face in the mirror, granting her the permission she sought. I watched as her hand slid open the medicine cabinet, removing a single razor blade from the unused box. She gripped the shiny silver object with her thumb and forefinger. She didn't tremble. She didn't cry. She touched the cool metal to her wrist.

My mother, tugged awake by disturbing dreams of severed umbilical cords, lurched free of the tangled sheets, rushing in the semi-darkness towards the crack of light beneath the bathroom door. She slammed it open, screaming at the situation she sensed, more than saw.

"No! Stop. Please, oh, God, please, don't do it!"

The razor blade slipped from my fingers and fell into the spotless white basin. She seized my wrists, her terrified eyes searching for the slashes.

"Why?" she had wailed."Why?"

Jerking my unblemished wrists from her grip, my bones turned to dust under the crushing avalanche of shame and remorse, I dropped to my knees, covering my face. She crouched beside me, holding me in her arms, rocking me like an infant, while she shook uncontrollably. With each gasping breath, she had squeezed a little tighter, crushing my matted head to her chest, filling my ears with the rabbit's pace pounding of her heart. We stayed huddled in the tiny white room until the sun broke over the rooftops, spilling through the lace curtains onto the floor. My hands, no longer reaching for death, lay curled and damp against my savior's shoulder. Love had pulled me back to Earth, back to my mother, back toward life.

Dr. Davison stood, tapping lightly on the face of her wristwatch, and I pulled my coat on. As I left the office, I stopped for a moment to look at the framed picture above Dee Davison's desk again. Leaning close to the glass and tilting my head so that I could see around the squiggly worm-like trails of blood seeping into the vitreous fluid of my eye, I recognized the artist's subject.

"It's an interesting depiction of Jesus, isn't it?" Dr. Davison said.

I lifted my head further, avoiding another blood worm swimming across my field of vision and considered the face in the frame. His head was tipped back, mouth open wide, rowed with tiny white teeth.

"He's screaming," I said."You're right. That *is* an unusual rendition."

"Screaming?" she said, "He's not screaming, Amy. He's laughing."

I furrowed my brow at the gaping mouth, at the curled lips, at the odd facial expression. Like the grease paint smile of a circus clown, the lines of despondency leaked through the laughter, revealing the truth behind the lie. Perhaps the doctor's interpretation was flawed. Maybe the artist had intended to convey Christ's rage. With all of the horrors that had been committed in his name, Jesus had more than a millennium worth of reasons to scream. There was five hundred years worth of reasons woven into the fabric of American history alone. Dr Davison probably didn't study history, though.

I turned away from the picture, not wanting to get into a discussion of Jesus or America's genocidal history. I had just failed a Christian psychologist's equivalent of a Rorschach ink blot test.

"Same time next week?" I asked, eager to escape the stuffy office, the stunned doctor, and the jovial Jesus.

"Yes," she said, after a long pause, "Same time next Wednesday."

The wind gusted as I left the building and climbed into my mother's warm car. Beneath the bare tree, the bits of brown still flew; their identities remained unknown.

CHAPTER TWELVE

WINTER OF THE BROKEN ROPE

The bitter January wind prowled the perimeter of the house, sneaking in through the cracks and crevices, its mournful whine a bleak reminder of the solemnity that accompanies darkness. Icy flecks of snow rose phantom-like from the crests of drifts, swirling on the forceful gusts and sounding like grains of sand against the window panes. Fresh new flakes fell from the black sky, visible only in a narrow pillar shed by the distant street lamp when the white-out conditions allowed light to escape through the storm. Chilled by the memory of the story my grandmother had shared of Clarence Howe's untimely demise, I shivered, pulling a crocheted afghan tighter around my shoulders.

I had not thought of the unfortunate farmer since my childhood, but the faded images that Grandma's tale had created so many winters ago floated to the surface once more: a flickering kerosene flame in the distance; bone-biting cold ripping at the horrified face of a man who realizes his life line has unraveled; a barrier of blowing snow obscuring the last pinpoint of illumination; a rotted rope tethered to a frozen corpse.

Although I remained curled in the corner of the sofa, the aged but sturdy walls of my family home protecting me from the storm, my awareness of the misgivings he must have experienced as he tentatively stepped away from the tiny glint of warmth and security in the window and into the tempest swirled through me. Neither the glow of the television nor the dim spot of the dining room lamp provided reassurance as I tilted my head in an effort to detect their light with my damaged left eye. I covered it with my palm and opened the other eye wide, already knowing the result. Nothing. Darkness.

***

I had lost the last remnants of light perception in October. Uncovering the left eye, I again tilted and turned my face towards the two sources of light. They appeared hazy and dull, but I exhaled the breath I had been holding in fearful anticipation, and felt a great sense of relief at their presence, regardless of the fact that the light was minimal. Light meant hope, for me as well as for my family, as we still grieved the loss of sight in my right eye and awaited the fate of my left. I smiled, brushing my hand over the surface of the coffee table in search of my mug of hot tea while recalling my grandparent's joy a month earlier when I told them that I had removed the bandages and had been able to see the twinkling strands of Christmas lights that adorned the tree.

"I knew everything was going to be all right. Didn't you, Lynn?" Grandma Bonnie had said, her voice full of strength and determination, as my grandfather nodded and embraced me, his chest quivering and his cheeks damp against mine.

I considered my grandmother's proclamation as I realized the tea had grown cold. I put the cup back on the table. Was "all right" the shadow land of muted light, indiscernible shapes, and unrecognizable faces in which I now found myself? Did my ability to see the Christmas tree lights, when I was unable to see the tree on which they were hung, fall under the definition of "all right"? If the regret I felt in leaving the University of Iowa without a degree in my hand, parking my car, not yet paid for, never to drive it again, and watching my friends desert me one by one as my condition worsened were considered "all right", then the expectations I associated with the word were too high.

The thin string of glimmering white specks seemed too fragile a tether to the visual realm of color, light, and shape. Perhaps the residual sight was a gift, for hadn't someone once said in the world of the blind, the one-eyed man is king? But I did not live in the world of the blind. I currently resided in a strange kind of no man's land where I served as an acceptable ambassador between the sighted world and the darkness that those who could see dreaded so much.

The loud crack of an ice-encrusted limb breaking from the maple tree startled me from my thoughts and returned my attention to the blizzard's intensity. The temperature kept dropping with the continuing storm and the chilliness crept into the house. I uncurled myself from the couch and stood, stretching my cramped legs and focusing once again on the dining room lamp in hopes that it would help me find the wall thermostat. But the light's appearance had changed. The dim glow of the bulb now seemed to be flanked by black velvet curtains slowly drawing closed as the light in the foreground faded like the gradual turning of a dimmer switch.

I stood frozen, an audience of one, watching in horror. In the length of a breath, the last thread of illumination disappeared, taking the blurred skyline of the no man's land with it into the folds of darkness as I crossed the border and entered into the world of the blind.

I squeezed my lids shut for several seconds in hope that eye strain was the culprit and that when I opened my eye again the light would return. Upon opening my lids, I saw only the murky charcoal gray that filled my vision like muddy marsh water, cloudy and flat.

I pressed my fist to my face, rubbing the sensitive tissue until the lid grew red and irritated and my eyeball throbbed. My attempts to blink, rub, and shake the shadows away having failed, I stood motionless, hands at my side, in defeat. The light was gone.

The blizzard lulled and I imagined myself somewhere within its cold embrace, the rope detached, the flicker of hope an unattainable memory, the desire to lay my exhausted body down among the white pillows of drifted snow flooding me with comforting resignation. The illusion of peace I found in knowing that my struggle was over dulled the severity of my situation as flashes of the recent past flickered through my mind: the hot needle-like pricks caused by the laser's futile attack on the leaking blood vessels of my diabetes-damaged retina; the gruesome sensation of post-operative sutures protruding from the white of my eye and brushing the back of the lid with every movement; the snipping sound as the nurse prepared me for cornea and retinal surgery, my long lashes falling from the shears and fluttering against my cheek like the ghosts of butterflies before they fell to the floor. Now, with the possibility of these memories physically manifesting into my life again gone, they, along with the scars of the flesh, could diminish over time.

My composure did not last, however. The storm, gathering momentum after its brief lull, sent winds whipping against the house, causing the wood siding to pop and crack under the onslaught. The storm door, unlatched by a sudden blast, slammed against its frame; urgency and panic began to race through me.

What if this is not the end? Maybe there is still time. Maybe, if I can get to an emergency room, they can help me, I thought, the magnitude of my condition shaking loose any thoughts of relief.

I lunged forward, fueled by the kind of terror that mounts with each tick of the clock, my shin slamming the edge of the oak coffee table, toppling the mug and splashing cold tea onto the carpet. Fire shot up and down my leg and I swore, clutching the wound as I stumbled to the floor. Ignoring the trickle of blood I felt creeping down the front of my leg, I tried to determine my location. The fall and the adrenalin coursing through my veins left me disoriented, and I cried with frustration, lost in a room that I had known for twenty-two years.

The wall phone seemed an unfathomable distance from where I sat, the ache of my shin reminding me of the end tables, the dining room chairs, the lamps, and the glass-front china cabinet that lay between myself and the kitchen. I rose on hands and knees, my fingers splayed in the thick carpet, absorbing the recollections its worn fibers revealed. This was the floor on which, with the coaxing of my maternal uncles, John, Matt, and Andy, along with several bottles of Coca-Cola, I had learned to walk. I had also learned to dance here. On rainy Saturday mornings, my imitations of American Bandstand moves brought laughter and applause from my mother, as she stood in the doorway watching my rendition of a disco hustle. But this night I would not dance across the floor, nor would I even walk. This night I must crawl.

On all fours, I moved in the direction I thought might lead to the phone, my hands searching for the end of the carpeting and the beginning of the smooth varnished hardwood planks of the dining room. My knee found the pool of tea and my jeans soaked up the cold liquid as my shoulder grazed the coffee table. It was the ringing of the phone that alerted me to its location and I crawled toward the sound. My knees bruised on the hard surface of the hallway, and, as I got to my feet, I groped the wall for the receiver, knocking the message board off kilter and sending pieces of chalk flying.

"Amy, its Mom. I was worried about you. I know your Dad and Sandy are out for the evening and the storm's getting worse."

With white knuckles and damp palms, I clutched the phone, unable to speak. My breath ragged, I could not form the words I knew would bring disappointment and despair to her as well as to the rest of my family. I swallowed and exhaled an audible breath.

"Something's wrong with my eye," I said, my voice hollow and unfamiliar.

"What is it? Does it hurt? Can you still see?"

"No, I can't see."

"What about light? Can you see light?"

"No."

I slumped against the wall, pressing my forehead to the cool yellow surface, nodding in silence as my mother's voice, choked with tears, instructed me to wait by the phone. She would send help.

Help arrived in the form of a red 4-wheel drive Jeep and the three men who had once taught me to walk. They piled into the cramped back porch, their brows, mustaches, and beards encrusted with frost, their faces crimson from the sub-zero wind. Three sets of gentle hands wrapped a scarf around my head, pulled a coat around my shoulders, and tied the laces of my boots. With Matt holding one of my arms and Andy the other, I stumbled out into the storm. Icy pellets of snow pelted my face, making it impossible to inhale the frigid air, and I felt the knee-deep drifts tugging at my boots as John guided me into the vehicle's warm interior.

The ferocity of the blizzard, not fully recognized within the Lake Park city limits, became apparent as we journeyed the thirty-five miles to Spencer along the deserted blacktops of the countryside. The Jeep swayed from the arctic blasts and the drifts reached out of the shallow ditches across the narrow road like monstrous ivory claws, scraping at the tires and the underside of the vehicle. We rode in silence, the danger that surrounded us oddly secondary to the knowledge my uncles and I contemplated about my current condition. Matt, a Wisconsin internist, knew it from a medical standpoint, Mom having consulted with him about my procedures, medications, and surgeries. Although ophthalmology was not his field of expertise and it was not he who had diagnosed or treated my diabetic retinopathy, he struggled to maintain his faith in the science of medicine as he watched the niece he had held in his arms as an infant lose her vision.

Andy had known it since the early stages, when, the previous summer, poor night vision prevented me from seeking a job outside of Lake Park. He and Aunt Connie needed daycare for my cousins, Amanda and Ben, and I, grateful for the opportunity, spent the long hot Midwestern afternoons among Ninja turtles and Barbie dolls. Every two weeks, I received more laser treatments, and then returned with less visual acuity, never admitting it to anyone. I feigned absent-mindedness, telling Amanda that I had left my eyeglasses at home and asked her to read the small print on the board games we played together. Claiming that I wanted to get more exercise, I parked my car and rode my bike the short distance to their house. I did not want to deceive anyone, but I didn't want to confess how quickly my sight was fading, either. When autumn arrived, Ben and Amanda returned to elementary school. Unable to read the textbooks' print, and finding it too hazardous to ride a bicycle any longer, I withdrew from college.

John perhaps understood my struggle on a more intimate level than his brothers, for he had been my companion and care giver. A car accident had temporarily left him in a halo brace following extensive back surgery and we had spent the previous two months recuperating together. When venturing out, I, with my protective metal eye patches and he, with a hard plastic ring, steel bolts protruding from it, encircling his skull, brought sympathetic glances, gaping-mouthed stares, and unwanted questions.

"Were the two of you in the same accident?" the video store clerk had asked, as she cracked her gum and tapped her neon pink nail tips against the counter.

Without answering, John had taken my arm and led me out onto the sidewalk. Inquisitive people often had the uncanny knack of insinuating reproach towards my uncle and me: he was the "bad" driver and I was the "bad" diabetic. We quickly learned to dodge their bullets of blame, however, playing the lead roles of the dark comedy that our lives had become with as much sardonic humor as possible.

The battles behind closed doors were shared as well. John witnessed the rapid decline of my right eye, his steady hand applying medication to the permanently dilated pupil, the once blue iris turned an ugly grayish-green, and the white tissue veined with scars and broken vessels. I heard his grunts of frustration and discomfort as he searched for a position that would let him rest within the hot, itchy confinement of the unyielding back brace. We were two battered warriors waiting in limbo for our fates to unfold: for the halo brace's removal to reveal movement or paralysis, for the gauze and metal eye patch's removal to reveal sight or blindness.

Daydreams of silvery scaled walleye dancing on the end of his fishing line filled John's head, the black and white photographic image of a crumbling stone wall I had once shot with my 35 mm camera on a sunny winter afternoon filled mine, and the longing for the slivers of memory to become possibilities for our futures filled us both.

The Jeep slowed, maneuvering the icy curves, as we entered the outskirts of Spencer. John's hand clasped my shoulder with a brief reassuring squeeze. Turning to face me in the darkness, his head no longer immobile, the halo brace gone, John's voice was low and rough as gravel.

"I love you, Kins."

Kins, short for Wollikins, was a nickname my uncles had given me at birth when they saw my full head of dark hair. He had not used the name in almost two decades.

I nodded, unable to answer him, as the snow crunched under the braking tires on the deserted side street outside the ophthalmologist's store front office.

When Dr. Barton, the on-call specialist, blew out a long breath through his thin pale lips and addressed my mother, rather than me, following the examination. I closed my eyes, the all-too-familiar sterile perfume of antiseptic and latex lingering in my nostrils like gun smoke, and let go. I let go of the last frayed thread of possibility, I let go of the flickering mirage of light. I let go of the idea that I would ever see again.

The tiny examination room seemed to expand around me and I, trapped in its center, listened to the voices from its perimeter, filtering through the vast space as fragmented whispers.

"Retinal detachment ..."

"Severely scarred ..."

"Major hemorrhaging ..."

"What now?"

"... more surgery?"

"Less than a slim chance ..."

"I am sorry."

And then the whispers ceased. Strong arms and gloved hands lifted and guided me out, the wind seizing the door's brass bell and crashing it violently against the glass as we exited. Suddenly, I could no longer walk and I stopped short, the screams building behind the prison bars of my head searching for a voice.

"It's too dark in here."

I want out."

"I can't get out."

"No, no, no!"

"Somebody help me!"

"There's no way out of here!"

"Help me!"

The family encircled me, their hunched shoulders and warm breath brushing my face. I shook my head, trying to dislodge the stifled screams and the suffocating blackness. But my scream could not free itself, and as falling snowflakes filled the midnight sky, I fell with them.

PART II

ECLIPSE

We live in the shadow of the real world.
-Tasunk Witko - Crazy Horse

1992

The rabbits danced on the snow· under a huge white moon. Somewhere, far away, my grandfather called my name, his voice growing louder, drawing closer. I resisted, not wanting to return to the other world. In that world, the rabbits no longer danced, the moon had vanished, and the dream had become the nightmare, the nightmare in which only sound existed, detached from its source, the incarcerating darkness converting my body into a windowless cell. But his voice was too close now; even if I could run, the rabbits ran faster. There was no choice but to open my eyes and allow the ghastly nothingness to press down, forcing the blind woman, dreaming of sight, to become the once sighted woman trapped in a blind waking terror.

After my collapse outside the doctor's office, January had passed, leaving few memories behind it. Someone had driven me to my grandparent's house. Someone had taken me up the narrow staircase. Someone had tucked me into the old metal bed beneath the fading wallpaper flowers of the dormer ceiling. I remembered nothing. But the brutal cold of February arrived, bringing with it pain so excruciating it wrenched my mind loose from the merciful oblivion. During the last surgery, a bubble of gas had been pumped into the interior of my eye in order to keep the retina from tearing or detaching, but it failed to accomplish its assigned task. Instead, it expanded and caused the eye pressure to climb until it exceeded six times the normal level. Only descriptions offered by chronic migraine sufferers could come close to describing the physical result. Certain that my skull would split from the force, I writhed, screamed, and vomited my stomach empty, retching violently until I lost consciousness. When I came to, I was sprawled on an examination table, Mom on one side, Grandpa Lynn on the other. They held my arms as a sterile male voice told me that what was about to happen would hurt. At that point, a bullet to my head would have been an acceptable solution, had it been the only available option, and I just nodded in listless agreement, figuring the twinge of his technique would pale in comparison with the existing agony. He ripped the plastic wrapper off a sterile syringe and jerked the cap from the needle, triggering memories of the sweet relief of the recent post operative Demerol injections. I imagined for a moment that the warning he had issued was only the prick of a hypodermic needle full of some wonderful narcotic. I was wrong. Terribly, terribly wrong.

"This will relieve some of the pressure," he said, carefully prying the lids apart."Hold very still."

His intentions became clear a split second too late and a short shocked huff was the only protestation I could manage as he inserted the needle directly into my eyeball. As warned, it hurt like hell, but the sickening sensation had been secondary to the sound it produced. When he drew back on the plunger, a high pitched whine, like air slowly releasing from the stretched neck of a balloon, squealed, as if my punctured eye was deflating. My mother clutched a hand to her mouth, stifling a gag. Grandpa Lynn sucked in his breath, took her by the shoulders, and moved her away from the table. My mind broke loose and escaped back into darkness. I felt as if my very spirit had been left behind in the barrel of that syringe.

Hours or perhaps days or perhaps weeks flowed by following that barbaric, but effective, treatment, and I slept, but didn't rest. I ate bits of food that I couldn't taste. I didn't shower, didn't brush my teeth, didn't comb my hair. In the little room with dresser drawers stuffed full of used wrapping paper and crumpled bows my grandmother intended to use again, but never would, and musty suit coats and chiffon dresses hung beneath their plastic shrouds in the closet, waiting in vain for another formal occasion that would never arrive, I stayed, quiet and still among my family's collection of things no one had the heart to discard. And as the begonia that had been rescued from the front porch after the first hard freeze dropped its dead leaves onto the floor in the corner, I existed. But I did not live.

The shock, followed by panic that initiated each new dawn, shoved me closer towards madness. Morning after dreaded morning, my grandfather climbed the stairs. Morning after dreaded morning, he woke me from dreams of light and color. Morning after dreaded morning, I slammed open my eyes to find, like Poe's Fortunato, that the final stone of my catacomb had long since been mortared into place. Cramped inside, with only the darkest thoughts to occupy time as I served my life sentence, I contemplated death, hating myself for the failed suicide attempt, resenting my mother for having stopped it. A thousand torturous twisted thoughts entangled with a thousand distorted disturbing memories choked my mind like thorny vines, squeezing out everything else. But as I huddled on one side of the wall, too weak and beaten down to even imagine escape, the people who loved me chipped away at the other side.

The money lenders, banks, and bill collectors had not disappeared along with their daughter's eye sight; life's continuing responsibilities kept my parents busy. Taking time off to stay home and care for me wasn't an option, so I remained with my retired grandparents. Grandpa and I sat together on the couch during the long afternoons and he was the one who rocked me as I sobbed against his shoulder. He never tried to convince me that everything was going to be all right; he had no expectations of comforting me with something I couldn't hold as truth. Petting my snarled greasy hair, he just held on and let the tears work their healing magic.

Every day, Grandma prepared the only foods I would eat: hot tea, soup, and soda crackers. Alarmed by my weight loss, she listed all the tempting dishes she was willing to cook, but I shook my head, my appetite disregarding the menu of all my favorites. Grandpa and Uncle John tested my blood glucose levels and measured insulin doses, only two of the many tasks I could not accomplish for myself. During the snowy winter evenings, I sat with my family in my semi-catatonic state as they gathered around the television to watch figure skating and ice dancing, Grandma's favorite Olympic events. John and Grandpa enjoyed them, too, but for quite different reasons. Grandpa liked the "cute little gals in the short costumes" and John, blessed with an irreverent sense of humor, delighted in the skaters' accidental falls and renamed their jumps and spins.

"Now that's *got* to hurt!" John chuckled sardonically as we all watched pair skating one night."A girl just did a Flying Butt Scissor and her partner caught her with the famous Austrian Ass Grab, but he dropped her and she slid with her skirt up around her waist. Now that's gold medal stuff!"

Grandpa sniggered and said, "Look at that! Her rear end slid right towards the camera. I think you should call that one the Moon Raker."

Grandma tried to keep a straight face as they lampooned her beloved sport, but finally gave in to a fit of guilty giggles."You two are terrible!" she scolded.

I hadn't said much that evening. Slouched in the corner of the sofa, I had tuned out most of the conversation and, as had become my routine, was lost in my own thoughts as I petted Grandma's miniature schnauzer. Bubbles lay with her bearded little chin pressed to my leg.But the mention of something called Flying Butt Scissors had caught my attention and, despite the strange inhibition that told me that my state of affairs was too dire for humor of any kind, a hint of a smile broke, hauling up the corners of my mouth.

"Do you remember that movie?" I said suddenly, my unexpected comment taking them off guard."The one about the blind ice skater. Do you remember it?"

John reluctantly admitted that he did.

I knew Grandma did, too, but she didn't say anything. Grandpa just shifted uncomfortably in his chair.

"The story took place in Iowa," I continued."She's a champion, but she falls and hits her head, loses her sight. Then she locks herself up in a little room and her boyfriend, played by Robbie Benson, I think, convinces her she can skate again." I started to laugh. It sounded bizarre, almost maniacal, but it felt good. Startled by my enthusiastic hand gestures, Bubbles stood up and jumped off the couch. I went on with the story."So she agrees to his ridiculous plan and learns how to skate blind. *Blind!* Can you believe that shit?"

No one answered, so I ranted on like the boisterous drunk who never takes notice of the way the person on the bar stool next to him is wincing.

"Her big comeback performance arrives and Robbie Benson leads her out onto the ice. The crowd is silent. Then the music starts. It's that song that everyone sings at weddings now. You know the one. Something about 'eyes' and 'love.'"

Rolling mine beneath bruised lids, I laughed harder, almost stopped, but pushed on, driven by some crazy need to finish."She skates this perfect routine; spins and leaps and probably even a Flying Butt Scissor or two. It's flawless! The crowd goes wild and Robbie's all choked up."

Grandpa excused himself at that point and retreated to the kitchen. My sides ached with laughter. Grandma and John were quiet.

"There's one little thing that the super blind skater and Robbie forgot!" I said, tears streaming down my red face, crazy bursts of laughter disjointing the words."The roses! They forgot the God damn roses!"

The triumphant scene had ended with the fans throwing long stem roses onto the ice for their blind heroin. As she glides around the rink, taking her bows, her blades hit the unexpected obstacle and she lands on her hands and knees. Robbie Benson runs to her aid and the crowd falls silent.

"If you ever expect me to skate professionally," I choked, still giggling, "don't let my fans throw any fuckin' flowers!"

Grandma and John seemed as stunned as the movie extras watching from the rink stands as Robbie brushed ice shavings off his humiliated girlfriend. Alone in my mirth, the laughter dwindled, then died. A unanimous disappointed "ah" rose from the television as another Olympian faltered on the ice. Grandma gripped the chair arms.

"I'm going to go help your grandfather with the dishes," she mumbled.

Her exit caused the last remnant of a smile to fade from my face and I slumped back into the corner of the couch, shrinking back from the catacomb wall that blocked me from the outside world. It was the first time since losing my sight that I had used the word, the first time I had referred to myself as "blind". I never would have planned or expected the moment to come in a mad outburst of dark humor. Apparently, my grandparents had not expected it, either, and hearing me poke at what seemed like a still very raw wound made them ill at ease. Perhaps Grandpa had been thinking of his skates hanging on a nail in the basement, the ones he wore when I was little, the ones he wore when he taught me how to skate a figure eight on the frozen surface of Silver Lake.

As I launched images of a fallen blind skater, Grandma may have been recalling the prior day, when she had witnessed the frustrated look on my face as I groped around on my hands and knees searching for a dropped sock. Battling with the decision of whether to pick up the lost item or to step back, she must have thought of all the dropped socks that would fill my future. In time, they would allow themselves to join me in the curative laughter, but, for now, only the clank of plates and silverware and the hiss of running water drifted from the kitchen. Uncle John cleared his throat. I had forgotten he was still there.

"Figure skating isn't your sport," he said, a grin forming on his stubbly cheeks.

I lifted my chin and raised an eyebrow.

"You're a ski jumper!"

A broad smile elevated my entire face and I could feel the laughter building up, spilling over.

"Are you going to coach me?"

He chortled in his devilishly ironic and delightfully infectious manner, lowering his voice conspiratorially for satiric effect. "Of course! Who could exploit the talent of their blind niece better than me? Robbie Benson?"

I laughed harder, spurring on his derisive comedy routine.

"Even if you wanted Robbie, he's not available. Strictly figure skating with a little rose gardening in the off season."

As his fantastical story took shape, our uproarious laughter brought Grandma from the kitchen and we shared our mock plan.

"Dad won't mind if we build a ski jumping slope off the roof of the garage, will he, Mom?" John asked with such a serious tone, I fell over on the couch, my belly shaking.

Grandma rolled her eyes in the same way she probably had thirty years earlier when she had discovered him leaning a ladder against the side of the house, the family cat, harnessed into a make-shift parachute, under his arm.

"Are you planning on taking up the sport?"

He shook his head and said, "Oh, no, much too dangerous! Amy's going to try it!"

John and I really cracked up then, braying like the jackasses Grandma, who wasn't laughing at all, probably figured us for.

"Don't worry, Grandma. It'll be perfectly safe," I chimed in. "We're going to put a giant net at the end. I'll fly right into it!"

John added, "She'll be the world's greatest blind ski jumper!"

She cringed. The "B" word had disturbed her when I said it, but it mortified her as, for the first time, someone else did. She wanted to scold John, wanted to point out his insensitivity, but suddenly recognizing he had connected with me in a way she was not ready to, let her look of horror melt away.

She hesitated, and then said, "Laughter is good medicine, isn't it?"

"And cheaper than really good narcotics," John said and I busted up again.

In the wall separating me from the outside world, a crack had formed between the stones and, on the other side, stood my Uncle John. The others had helped him chip away at the mortar, using their love, their care, their sympathy, but it was the empathy in his and my laughter that broke through the barrier. Perhaps it was the time he had spent in his own prison, after the car accident and the surgery when his head, neck, and back were locked in the steel brace. Maybe he wished we would have laughed more when he had made jokes about the screws in his forehead and the metal halo surrounding his skull. Maybe it would have made it easier if we could have been more comfortable with his references to Frankenstein and cyborgs. But whether born of his experience or from an innate gift to know when even the most serious situation should be taken less seriously, Uncle John got it.

In the middle of the longest and shortest month, my father came to visit. Grandpa and Grandma welcomed him at the kitchen door with smiles, hugs, and a cup of hot coffee. The warmth between them hadn't been extinguished by my parents' divorce and he greeted his former in-laws as long-time friends. Dressed and showered for the first day in many days, I sat at the window listening to the wind blow flecks of snow against the pane and the chickadees singing their own names as they picked the millet and safflower seed from the frost on the feeder tray. Dad sat down beside me and watched the birds for a moment before he spoke.

"I see the red polls are down from the north."

I nodded.

"The nuthatch is out there, too. He's upside down on the box elder trunk."

With a shadow of a smile and the strong need to show him that I was no longer cut off from the world, I said, "The chickadees are here, too."

"Happy Valentine's," he said softly, sliding a wrapped box towards me."This is for you."

I touched the gift's ribbon bow tentatively. He and I had not celebrated the holiday since I was a child when the construction paper hearts, with their glitter and paste and crayon, were still signed to "Daddy".

"Open it," he said nervously.

With deliberate care, I peeled the bow loose and unwrapped the gift without tearing the pink tissue paper. When the box was bare I paused, afraid of the way my father's sentiment might make me feel if I ripped the final pieces of tape away and accepted whatever lay inside.

"Do you need some help?" he asked.

I shook my head and slowly pulled my fingernail across the taped flaps, unsealing the box. A sweet scent floated from inside and I moved more tissue paper aside to reveal a papier-mâché heart. I lifted it from the box and held it in both hands, rubbing its texture.

"It's covered with painted roses. And if you lift the lid," he said, reaching over and gently tugging the top half of the heart free, "inside, there's dried flowers. They have a pretty smell. I thought because …."

He couldn't say it and he retraced his steps. The idea that had, at its conception, seemed so considerate, suddenly seemed insensitive as he watched my fingers tracing the heart's outline, my eyes never opening.

Well, I just thought you might like it," he finished.

Lifting the open heart, I breathed in the potpourri's rose perfume and traveled back to Grandpa Jack's patio where the bleeding hearts had once grown, where on that day years ago he had cut the fragile flowers, sending them along with the ignited spark born of his revelation, the revelation of his blood, my father's blood, my blood. The heart in my hands reminded me of that connection, the connection of blood that brought the strength of generations of proud Indian people, the connection that brought the disease from my father to me, the connection that had left me in the darkest darkness. Our hearts pumped the memories of the ridiculed boy who carried his indoctrinated self-hatred into old age. It flowed full of my father's remorse for his diabetic child. Our blood, with all that it carried, ended within me, for better or for worse.

Remembering the hardships survived by my grandfather, and the physical and emotional distress endured, without complaint, by my father, I felt sure it was for the better. The tenacity and fortitude of warriors were my legacy. The spark of primal power was my legacy. Blindness could steal the sun. It could rob the moon and stars from the night. But it couldn't take the spark, the spark that contained my spirit.

"Thank you," I said."It's beautiful."

He slid the cover onto the heart, making it whole again before he kissed my cheek and went out into the early dusk. The birds were taking flight, returning home for the evening. In the western sky, the sun dogs continued their chase around the setting white light.

CHAPTER THIRTEEN

SPRING OF WHITE CANES

"Ready?"

I wondered if Mitchell understood the implications looming in his question as I took the gift he offered. Without answering, I stood like a blind warrior, prepared for battle, a long white fiberglass cane held in my fist like a spear. Having acknowledged the cane and all it represented, I felt myself pulled through a portal, traveling between worlds. Silently bidding farewell to the woman and the life I had known, I left both, like a shed skin, in the downtown Minneapolis parking lot, and prepared to fight my way through the dark.

The metallic click of Mitchell's cane tip against the asphalt quickened my pulse as he moved towards the roar of Hennepin Avenue and I realized that I was expected to follow. I positioned the grip in my sweaty palm and concentrated on his boot thuds and cane taps. Frantically, I tried to remember the abbreviated lesson he and his friend, Daniel, had given me the previous day when I had been introduced to them and the white cane. My experiences with blind people up to that point had been limited to a woman who my mother had delivered hot meals to when I was a child. She never left her dingy mobile home, reeked of booze, and cursed at any further offers of help. My other example was a camp counselor. She had busted my bunk mates and me for sneaking off the grounds. The sound of soda cans being secretly popped open after lights out had alerted her to our earlier illegal excursion to the general store a mile down the road.

Having only recollections of an abusive alcoholic and the amazing young woman with the canine-like hearing as references, prior to meeting Mitchell and Daniel my trepidation mounted. But on arrival at Mitchell's home, I was relieved to find very pleasant and welcoming young men. Mitchell, an eager college student, immediately took me, a fledgling of the blind community, under his wing. Moments after our introduction, he launched into details about independent living skills. Unlike Mitchell, who had been born blind, Daniel had received the best solutions that the Johns Hopkins ophthalmology team had to offer, but, in the end, had, like me, lost the battle with diabetic retinopathy. He attended the rehabilitation center where Mitchell had received training and where I planned to soon enroll.

Hanging back, Daniel reflected on his choice of words, my presence seemingly a sudden reminder of how overwhelming the initial months of blindness are and of how much he had struggled to reach this point. Mitchell's no-nonsense description of computer training, Braille, and cane travel spurred hopes that, physically, I could overcome the limitations of my loss, but it was Daniel's selective comments and his carefully chosen moments of silence that spoke of higher hurdles, of deeper ditches.

"I really miss my car," he said later, when our host had gone to the kitchen for drinks."I gave my Honda to my brother and he's driven the hell out of it. Never even washes it."

I swallowed, remembering the red hatchback and the Sunday afternoons I had once spent cruising the rural gravel roads in search of subjects to capture on black and white film. The car no longer belonged to me. Neither did the camera.

"My stepfather bought mine, but he takes good care of it. Don't like to ride in it though. It feels too strange not to be at the wheel. I suppose I'll get used to it … eventually, but it's too new. Everything happened so fast."

He sighed, leaning back in the chair."It does happen too damn fast doesn't it? It seems like one day they were telling me I had diabetes; the next, they said I had retinopathy; and the day after that, I was stumbling around in the dark wondering how this happened."

He shook his head and a sardonic little laugh escaped. Suddenly, he grabbed the talking glucose meter that he had demonstrated earlier off the table and jammed it into its case.

"How'd you and I get so lucky? Each twenty-one, and life to go." He tossed a clicking device, used to fill syringes, into the case beside bottles of insulin. In a dark annex of my brain, an equation formulated, calculating the potential decades ahead in our sentences.

"Don't let Mitchell's gung ho approach sway you into thinking it's just about learning to swing a cane or read a Braille book. Sure, that's important, but there will be times when you are going to miss the sighted life. He can't empathize."

Zipping the case shut, he shoved it away."It's the difference between wishing and missing. On his bad days, he wishes for sight. On our bad days, we miss it. Like that dog that you have when you're a kid. You know, the one who always sleeps with you, curled up at the end of your bed, the one who's there wagging his tail when you come home."

His voice took on a dry, dead leaf quality."It's the dog that ran into the street just as a garbage truck flew around the corner and you couldn't do a damn thing to stop it. Mitchell never buried his fingers in that furry coat. Never felt that tongue on his face. He never knew that dog."

He grew quiet then, and we sat, observing our moment of silence, before the game of blind man's bluff began again. Mitchell rattled cubes in the ice maker, and Daniel released a long breath.

"Take it easy on yourself. You'll quickly learn the techniques. He's right about that. Training will only last about a year. But the things in your head and in your heart, the loss, the disappointment, the anger, those will last longer and be a hell of a lot tougher."

As I stood with feet glued to the concrete and panic radiating through me in nauseating waves, I thought of Daniel's words and could not imagine anything tougher than thrusting myself into the surrounding urban chaos.

"Are you coming?"

Mitchell had spun around and yelled from the sidewalk like a manic child at the gates of an amusement park, immune to the anxiety that riveted me to the spot.

"The rehab center's two blocks away. The director's expecting us for your consultation. Let's go!"

My mother spoke up, noting the perspiration that, in spite of the chilly March air, beaded my forehead, calling, "Maybe she should take my arm, Mitchell. There's a lot of traffic. I'd feel better if I could help."

Grateful for the way in which she had attempted to salvage my pride, I threw her an uneasy smile. He rushed back into the parking lot and I visualized him shaking his head, the red strands of the mullet my mother had described falling across his pale brow.

"No, that's not a good idea. You need to do it for yourself. When you start training, you'll be out here on your own every day. The instructor won't let you hold his hand."

"She's only been blind a month. Maybe it's too soon," she countered, a perturbed edge hinting at the approach of her mother lioness mode.

"What do you think?" he asked as he turned from my mother and addressed me."I'll go slow and you can follow the sound of my cane. The teacher's blind, too.When you begin instruction, you'll rely on his cane tap until you're confident with your own sense of direction. Just try it."He stepped forward."If it gets too bad, you can take her arm, but at least give it a shot."

I didn't move. Every ounce of courage lay buried beneath the overwhelming urge to scream, to cry, to begin flailing my fists at the invisible enemy that had inflicted this irreversible agony upon me. Where was the tiny Pekinese puppy my parents had gifted me with for my seventh birthday? She was long gone. Where was the rest of the world? Somewhere beyond this black curtain.

Mitchell's commanding tone softened."I know you're afraid. Everyone is at first. But, I promise, it gets easier. You can't give in to it."

I flashed then on the old woman in the trailer, her eyes hidden behind dark glasses, the rank odor of stale whiskey and a soiled housecoat the perfume of her misery. A razor blade, a joint, a bottle of vodka; in anguish, I had tried them all. Deep depression and the craving for instant relief lured me. I had not gone very far in those directions before I turned back, my spirit seeking less delusion-based, less destructiveforms of comfort. But fear could be a powerful opponent. It molded people's minds and shaped their identities. I had seen it in the faces of my kindergarten classmates when they shunned me on the playground because of my diabetes. I had seen it in my Grandpa Jack's boyhood stories of the boarding school nuns who had beaten the Lakota spirit from him.And I had seen it in the scowl of an embittered blind addict. Two routes lay before me and I could not let consternation choose my direction.

"I'll do it," I finally said, my hands trembling, my voice soft, yet resolute, as I inched towards the horns and motors of Hennepin Avenue.

Mitchell's faint cane tap veered left as we reached the edge of the parking lot and I shuffled behind his long strides, exploring the path and searching for obstacles with my feet, not yet sure of what my cane was communicating.

"Are you there?" I yelled, unable to judge the distance between us, suddenly certain that I had already lost him in the noise.

"Right here," he answered, surprising me with his proximity."I hear your dragging feet. Break that habit immediately. Pay attention to the cane's information. It alerts you to a curb or stairs more safely than your feet ever will. If you wait for your toe to find a steel sign post rather than letting the cane do it, you're asking for a broken nose. Understand?"

I nodded, forgetting that he could not see the gesture, but wondering if he, too, possessed the heightened super-senses of my former camp counselor.

"It's a common mistake, but I want to give you a head start on the basics."

We continued along the crowded street, Mitchell forging ahead, my mother, observing nervously from somewhere in the rear of our odd little procession, andI, baby stepping, but no longer shuffling, between them. Bus brakes squealed, police sirens wailed, and a jackhammer pounded its staccato beats, all instruments in the psychotic symphony of the city. The sounds assaulted my ears and awakened the primal instinct to crouch like a wild animal in the shadows of steel and concrete that loomed predatorily around us. My shoulder muscles began to ache and my legs cramped. Clenching my teeth, I attempted to filter out the distractive din while, at the same time, I labored to interpret the useful sounds that could save me from danger and embarrassment. The trek seemed endless.

"You're doing great."

My mother's voice stretched like a lifeline through the mayhem, her praise massaging some of the tension from my neck. I picked up my snail's pace, and closed in on Mitchell's footfalls. As my confidence grew, I adapted my posture, raising my chin. But the shining moment did not last, for the city, with all of its noise and clutter, was not going to let a blind small-town Iowa girl off that easily. Somewhere, a siren suddenly screamed above the existing noise. It drowned out Mitchell's cane with its deafening wail, and drew nearer as a fire engine roared onto the avenue.My unaccustomed eardrums hurt. The sudden paranoid premonition that it was bearing down, about to crush us beneath its speeding wheels, rushed into my thoughts. Panic triggered the instinct for flight and I pivoted left, then right as I sought escape, but I could not break free. I lurched forward and bumped into someone.

"Excuse me. Sorry," I stammered, and sidestepped to avoid repeating the graceless maneuver.

I bloodied my knuckle against something metal.

"No harm done," a sympathetic masculine voice said."Are you looking for the bus stop?"

I shook my head and heat rushed to my cheeks as I felt my mother's familiar hand suddenly guiding me through the tangle of people and bus benches.

"Still with me?" Mitchell hollered from up the street."I figured you lost track because of the noise."

"Yes," I answered, fighting to steady my voice."I got hung up back here."

I leaned towards her, and lightly kissed my mother's cheek, whispering, "Thanks," as I released my arm from her grasp and made my way towards him.

"Travel in the center of the sidewalk. There's a lot of things to run into along the curb and next to buildings. So unless you're looking for a bus stop or a trash can, you should aim for the middle."

I snorted, teetering between the impulse to either hug him or hit him.

"Did anyone ever tell you that your timing is lousy, Mitchell?"

"Guess you must have found the Downtown 28 bus bench, huh?"

"Yeah, about a minute before you gave me your 'middle of the road' speech."

Unscathed, he nudged my toe with his cane tip."I bet you'll never forget where that bus picks up, will you?"

In the year ahead, as I rehabbed, I would repeatedly be given the opportunity to learn this teaching. Being but an infant in the world of the blind, I was afforded daily lessons in the delicate balance between humility and confidence. As I would quickly come to understand, ego must be discarded at the door of B.L.I.N.D., Inc., for it had earned its nickname, "Boot Camp for the Blind". My mistakes made as a beginning student were excellent teaching tools, not only for me, but for those who would come after in the program. Over time, I realized that a bruised ego attained during one experience could save someone a broken leg during another.

"You're going to learn how to cross the street," he announced as we approached an intersection."This is Fifth and it runs one way. Do you hear the cars idling on your left?"

"Yes."

"They're heading west. For the most part, Minneapolis streets run east and west. Avenues, north and south. There are some exceptions, like Franklin Avenue, but learning street directions can help you. Especially if you're lost.And trust me," he laughed, "you will get lost."

"Lost. What do you mean 'lost'?" my mother said, instinctively grabbing a wad of my jacket.

"Not lost in the sense of calling the police or filing a missing persons report. But sometimes, you'll get off the bus at the wrong stop or lose track of which street you've just crossed. It's common for new cane users to spend some time on an uptown bus when they intend to go downtown or walking along Marquette when the address they're looking for is on Third. I did. I still do sometimes. Drivers make wrong turns once in a while. Blind travelers do, too. We get distracted or we're tired or we have other things on our minds. You take a left when you should have taken a right. The difference is we don't have the advantage of sign posts, so we have to rely on other tools to help us find our way back onto the path."

She loosened her death grip on my jacket, but only slightly.

"I don't know if I feel any better about my daughter wandering around Minneapolis. It seems too risky."

In that moment, unlike any similar moment my mother and I had ever shared, her protective maternal instinct stood in defiance of my independence. Although she had freed my hand as I climbed on to the bus my first day of kindergarten, lifted her hold on the back of my bicycle during the first wobbly spin without training wheels, and, just three years prior to this moment, had waved as the car pulled away from the University of Iowa freshmen dorm, she could not command her fingers to relinquish the clump of jacket sleeve. What kind of mother would let go? What kind of mother could push her blind offspring from the nest into Fifth and Hennepin?

"It is risky," Mitchell said."Freedom carries risk. But you're not pushing a bird from a nest. You're releasing her from a cage."

She tried to reply, as, for a split second, she considered dragging me back to the car, locking the doors, and racing out of the city, but her words caught in her throat, suddenly seeming as nonsensical as the plan to spirit me away. Her hand shook, but she did let go. There wasn't an argument that could hold up against the simple truth. An independent life demanded more than just my courage. It required her courage, too.

I joined Mitchell at the curb and he demonstrated how to line up at the cross walk, "The most important part is listening to the flow of parallel and perpendicular traffic. When you hear the cars moving parallel to the cross walk, you go. But be cautious of the ones turning onto the street you're crossing. If the traffic is moving perpendicularly, you wait. All right, time for your first test."

Adrenalin raced through my veins and I quivered like a wired greyhound.

"Listen to a few cycles of traffic. When you think it's safe to cross, tell me."

I strained my ears, trying to decipher the jumble of mechanical motion. Eventually, I judged that the traffic was passing in front of us.

"I don't think it's safe," I said, a little uncertain of my choice.

"Right. That's good. Tell me when the light changes."

A truck's brakes whined several feet to the left, and the roar of engines increased to the right as the traffic began to move along Hennepin.

"Now?"

"Yeah, that's right!" he said, excited with his success as an amateur teacher and with the progress of his first pupil."After the next cycle, tell me when it's safe. Then your mom and I will cross."

"What about me?"

"Wait until the next green light and then cross."

"Mitchell, I don't think …," I started, but hesitated as the blind drunk's pinched face, filled with self-hatred and hatred for a world she could no longer see, drifted into my thoughts like a grim apparition.

"You don't think what?" he asked, poised at the edge of the curb.

"I don't think I've ever been more scared."

"Are you sure?" my mother asked, taking my fingers, lacing them in hers.

"Yes.I'll have to do it at some point. If I wait, it's not going to get less frightening"

"I wouldn't mind if you waited. In fact, as far as I'm concerned, you don't have to do it at all."

"I know, but you'd probably push me across in a stroller if I'd let you," I said, smirking at the ridiculous image."You'd take care of me forever and I love you for that, but that wouldn't be good for either one of us."

I unlocked my fingers from hers and gave her a gentle shove towards Mitchell."Besides, they don't make strollers that big, so I guess I'll just cross this damn street."

After several minutes of intense listening, I gave them the green light, holding my breath until I heard Mitchell's shout from across the polluted river of motion. A lifetime passed, or perhaps only a second, suddenly the two seeming one and the same, before the cars slowed to a stop on Fifth and the parallel traffic crawled forward, my pulse accelerating with it.

"It's safe to walk," someone said.

I thanked the man, whose presence I had not noticed before, and stepped off the curb. But the familiarity of the stranger's voice lingered. It unlatched a door in my mind. As my boot touched the pavement, his words still whispered like mystical incantations, time falling away with my fear, and I, cloaked in memory, was a small girl once more. The unyielding concrete no longer existed beneath my feet, magically replaced by the soft inviting weave of a carpet, my toddling toes, tiny and bare, curled against it. Across the great unknown space, I moved, legs shaking with every tentative step, and, ahead, they waited, my uncles, John, Matt, and Andy, their arms outstretched for their infant niece. I could hear them calling my nickname, the city's cold cry transformed into their gentle encouragement.

"You can do it, Kins! Just a few more steps!"

"That's it. Keep coming. Look what I have for you!"

My mouth watered in anticipation of the Coca-Cola bottle John held, and I grinned as Andy and Matt jiggled stuffed toys, the floppy beagle and bunny ears flapping like wings. The sweetness of the far off memory kept propelling me, until I reached the other side. Fifth Street roared to life, its horns and diesel engines tugging me back into the present. The image of my uncles' proud faces vanished among the clouds of automobile exhaust, replaced by Mitchell's cheers and whistles and my mother's embrace, as we celebrated the first one hundred yards in the undeterminable distance of my new journey.

CHAPTER FOURTEEN

SUMMER OF BLIND BOOT CAMP

Shouts and cheers echoed down the hall of the rehabilitation center and I lifted my fingers from the Faulkner short story I had spent most of the morning struggling to read. Eager to join the excitement in the lobby, I grabbed my cane and hurried towards the sound of applause and laughter. Bernie had returned, victorious, and the students and staff surrounded him as he gripped the handle of the antique school bell and proudly rang it. We applauded the tradition reserved for the successful completion of one of several challenging tasks that lead to graduation.

"I did it, baby," Bernie said, his voice breaking.

His wife, Paula, slid from behind the reception desk and threw her arms around his neck; their lips touched, tasting the tears of their joy. As the crowd dispersed, each person carrying a piece of Bernie's victory with them into their next class, I gripped his shoulder.

"Congratulations, Bernie. How did it go out there? What a lousy day for a drop-off."

He shrugged, wiped his face on his sleeve, and clicked back into his usual tough guy persona.

"Shit, Ames," he grinned, "it was a piece of cake. A little rain can't stop an old country boy like me."

"I don't know. The thought of getting dumped somewhere and having to find my way back, especially on a day like today, scares me. Hell, I still feel like I'm going to puke just walking alone to the bus stop."

Bernie laughed, and then suddenly turned serious."Your time is coming. It'll creep up on you quicker than you think. In fact, I heard Roger talking and he says you're getting dropped off tomorrow."

I frowned, panic rising as perspiration rose on my palms. Roger knew I wasn't ready for my first drop-off yet. Would he really send me out there so early in my training? It seemed extreme even for a cane travel instructor at the "Blind Boot Camp". I shook my head."No, you must have heard him wrong, Bernie."

"No, I heard him right. You, tomorrow, in the car, to the suburbs. They'll shove you out, and then you walk back. Simple as that. Better wear comfortable shoes, kid."

I shifted the white cane to the crook of my arm and wiped my damp hands on my jeans. I leaned against Paula's desk. She took pity on me and, rolling her eyes, intervened into Bernie's impish teasing.

"Come on, Bern, you know they aren't sending her out this soon. Give it a rest before she passes out on my desk."

He poked my arm with the handle of his cane and chuckled like a chastised schoolboy."Gotcha, didn't I? Just trying to toughen you up."

I playfully jabbed him in the bicep, embarrassed by my gullibility as well as my dismay.

"See, Paula, it's working. She's tougher already. I almost felt that."

"Don't let him trick you," Paula said."Superman here has his kryptonite moments, too. He just doesn't want anyone to know it."

She sat down to answer a phone call and I followed Bernie, tormentor, surrogate big brother, and friend, to the lunch room. I had grown to admire his mental as well as his physical strength in the months since my training began and it was hard to imagine him afraid, but Paula, better than anyone, understood the truth. She had been at his side through the entire horrifying and glorious journey, and had witnessed what lay beneath his steely exterior. Four years had passed since she received the phone call. The words "farm machinery accident,""critical condition," "last rites," unwound from the receiver, choking her like a noose. She clung to his hand as he drifted in and out of consciousness, death threatening to steal him, transfusion after transfusion pumping into his veins. When Bernie screamed at her from his hospital bed to get out and to find a "whole" man, she stayed.

"Do you think you're going to get out of marrying me that easy, you son of a bitch? I love you and I know you love me. Nothing is going to change that," Paula had said, her adamant refusal to leave eventually winning out over Bernie's abandonment issues.

She loved him through the suffering, the anger, the loss, and vowed never to allow the fate that had torn his legs from his body and blinded his eyes to rob them of their dreams. When the wounds of the flesh were healed, Bernie, with the aid of prostheses and a walker, stood at the altar beside his bride and honored the promise made in another lifetime.

Bernie and I stopped in the lunch room, killing time, neither of us eager to return to our designated classrooms. I dug in the pocket of my jeans for some change. He pulled his wheelchair up to the lunch table and slid his cane under it. I bought two sodas from the machine, offered Bernie a Coke, and sat down beside him. He took the can, cracking it open as he yawned. I wondered how far he had traveled from his drop-off point. It wasn't the piece of cake he described. Of that I was sure. The average location left the student three miles from the rehab center. Riding the bus back was not allowed and only one question could be asked of passers-by. The idea of it this early in my training truly terrified me and I smiled to myself, plotting a way to repay Bernie's little joke.

He stretched and yawned a second time. The event must have exhausted him, but he wouldn't complain. He never did. I wanted to compliment him again, to tell him how much his character inspired me, to further convey how much I respected him. But a lesson from the recent past flashed into my mind, warning of the lines that shouldn't be crossed, which signaled my caution.

A week earlier, we had been dining at a deli when a patron had approached Bernie. She gushed at him in a tone reserved for adorable children or cute puppies.

"You're so amazing. I can't believe how well you do, considering you don't have any—well, you know. And you can't see, either. That's just too incredible."

Unable to maneuver away in the crowded restaurant, Bernie smiled as he tried to keep his embarrassment in check. He turned his wheelchair, politely attempting to discourage her, but she didn't take the hint. She then called a co-worker over to "meet a real hero". The lunch crowd hushed, their attention drawn to the woman's boisterous praise. Bernie's reserve crumbled with each syllable, finally toppling as she, preparing to depart, patted him on the head. With clenched teeth, he swung around to face her.

"Praise like that is just another form of pity," he said, jerking his head from under her hand."And there's nothing that pisses me off more than someone pitying my blind legless ass while I'm trying to eat my fucking lunch."

The woman drew in an audible breath, her cheeks reddening, as her lips pursed. Like the flip of a switch, her voice lost its sympathetic warmth. Antagonism sharpened her words into weapons and she slashed at the already frayed threads of Bernie's dignity as she exited the deli.

"I guess it's acceptable to be rude and mean when you're handicapped," she said, spitting out the last word like a filthy punctuation mark.

The incident lingered in my memory as we sat in the lunch room drinking our sodas. I understood the humiliation of a verbal pat on the head. It happened to all of us. The white cane acted like a magnet, attracting the amazed, the curious, the condescending. Bernie's situation drew twice as much unwanted attention and he was forced to deal with an impromptu sideshow audience almost everywhere he went. I crushed the sides of my empty Diet Coke can. He deserved better.

Bernie reminded me of the men I had grown up with in rural Iowa: a masculine, hard-working, farm laborer who earned his living with muscle and sweat. His accident had stripped him of that identity, but he still held fast to the mentality. I remembered the weathered faces of the farmers that gathered at the grain elevator, asking each other's opinions about whether to buy or sell corn. I remembered the way a man stood a little taller when his neighbor asked what kind of beans he was going to plant that year. Turning to Bernie, the man who still wore blue jeans, pearl snap button shirts, and a faded John Deer cap, I molded the admiration, respect, and praise into an acceptable form of compliment and asked for his advice.

"I'm going to be cooking my large meal next week. Do you think I should do manicotti or lasagna?"

A discussion about pasta was a far cry from a man's opinion concerning seed corn or tractor tires, but, in the world in which Bernie and I currently resided, it garnered every bit as much importance. The large meal, like the drop-off, built confidence, and at its successful completion earned the student who prepared it a chance to ring the freedom bell. It was not as daunting a task to me as it was to some of the students. Years of apprenticeship in the kitchens of my mother and grandmothers rewarded me with knowledge and a comfort level with cooking that many students didn't have. But it still wouldn't be easy. All of the meals four courses were made from scratch, including the sauce and the bread. Grocery lists, shopping trips, serving, and clean-up all figured into the project. The thirty students and staff members served as dinner guests, requiring recipes be tripled, or even quadrupled, to accommodate everyone's appetites.

"What do you stuff your manicotti with?" Bernie said, straightening his shoulders against the chair's backrest.

"Ricotta cheese."

"Figure you're gonna have to stuff about a hundred. How fast can you sling ricotta? That's a hell of a lot of shells."

Bernie lobbed our empty cans into the recycling bin, banking them off the side of the vending machine. He made it all appear too effortless: traveling three miles through the rainy streets of Minneapolis, serving teriyaki stir fry to thirty-five guests, managing to find humor among the hardships. But a hundred manicotti shells would take a lot of time and toil and I wrinkled my brow at the thought.

"It's all about time management," he said, mimicking the household skill instructor's favorite phrase."Make the manicotti the day before. Refrigerate them overnight and bake your French bread the morning of the meal."

Bernie tapped his finger on the table."See? No sweat. Easy as one, two, three."

He lowered his voice a little, as if he might reveal the secrets of all his successes."Besides, a lot of people go the lasagna route. Sure, it's less work, but you're a damn good cook. Challenge yourself."

I smiled at the compliment, happy that our admiration was mutual."All right, manicotti it is then. I won't argue with the master. Thanks, Bernie."

He picked up his cane."You should get back to Braille class before they catch you goofing off. I gotta head to the computer room," he said with the pride and protectiveness of an older brother

I located my cane with my foot and hit my head on the chair as I reached for it, startled by George's grating voice.

"What are you two doing? Aren't you supposed to be in class?" he accused, blocking the entrance to the hall.

George never missed an opportunity to unleash his nasty disposition. He was a new arrival to the center and resented his state counselor's recommendation, entering into training with the purpose of making the process as unpleasant as possible. He argued that his residual sight was adequate and that learning Braille and cane travel was a waste of time. But his denial did not erase the fact that retinitis pigmentosa would someday destroy his remaining vision. After much prodding and cajoling, the counselor won the argument.

George, like a number of students, wore sleep shades. The dense black mask blocked out light, simulating complete blindness. Although they were hot and uncomfortable, they allowed him to learn without relying upon the distortions of his less than perfect eyesight. George hated the shades.

I attempted to slip past him, not wanting a confrontation, but he stepped towards the wall and halted my escape. He lowered his voice to an ugly whisper.

"Do you have your sleep shades on, Amy?"

I did not answer.

"Oh, that's right," he smirked."You don't need them. You're a total."

"Totals" and "partials" wereout-dated and derogatory terms once used to categorize institutionalized blind children according to their ability or inability to see. Children with residual sight, often granted privileges and responsibilities denied to those without sight, established themselves at the top of the hierarchy. They were fighting words in a rehab program designed to dispel negative stereotypes and promote equality. George knew it and he waited for my reaction, anticipating the chaos he had hoped to create with his cruelty. I pushed past him, unscathed by his pathetic assault.

"Are you going to tell the director on me?"

Unwilling to provide the twisted form of attention he craved, I ignored the question. But the insult had not gone unnoticed. Bernie rolled forward, and pinned him in the narrow hall.

"So we're totals, George? What does that make you?"

He squirmed, the empty foot rests of Bernie's chair gouging into his shins.

"You know what I think, George? I think you're a total."

Infuriation contorted his face and he shoved Bernie back, his yell disrupting classes and bringing curious students and staff into the hallway.

"I'm not a total," he raged, as he ripped the sleep shades off and hurled them to the floor."I can see! I'm not a goddamn total!"

"You are a total, George," Bernie said."You're a total asshole!"

George stormed into the men's room, slammed the door, and swore at Bernie. No one followed him. We had grown accustomed to his tantrums. They occurred daily and, if ignored, ended quickly. I retrieved the crumpled black mask from under Bernie's wheelchair and laid it on the lunch table.

The altercation was over and we returned to our classrooms.

The thick Braille copy of short stories lay open where I left it and I ran my fingers over the page, searching for the last sentence I read. Jane tapped the corner of the book with a metal slate.

"How many pages have you read this morning?"

"Four. That's not very good, is it?" I said.

"No, it is good. You're improving more every day," she said."I'd like you to finish ten pages by tomorrow's class."

I moved my hand slowly across the heavy paper, concentrating on the clusters of bumps. The meanings of each tactile symbol came at an agonizing pace. My mind strained, clumsy and unwilling to process the information my fingers, rather than my eyes, collected, as I wrestled with the mental transition.

Carlos, a South American student who had lost his sight in a motorcycle crash, came in and sat down at the table beside me. Jane handed him a metal slate and a stylus. Greeting us, he slid a piece of paper into the slate, preparing to take dictation. She selected a computer software manual from the rows of Braille books on the shelf and began reading a tedious paragraph containing many long words and number sequences. Her fingers glided over the material without faltering. She had learned the "mysterious dot language" when she was still a girl and had developed the center's adult Braille curriculum. After two sentences, Carlos stopped.

"Jane, I'm still on the first word," he said, frustrated and embarrassed."I can't write that fast yet."

The admission was raw. Carlos was in his thirties and, like most of us who had become blind as adults; he found learning to read and write again humbling at best and, at worst, humiliating. Jane suggested that he write a paragraph of his own creation to warm up. With Carlos working independently, she asked me to read aloud. I bristled at the request, dreading the sound of my own voice. The dots rose from the page like jagged stones and I stumbled over Faulkner's words, lost my place, stopped, and then started over. The story sluggishly unfolded. The lines issued from my lips, slow, soft, and uncertain, my voice no longer that of a woman, but of a little girl, uncovering the mystery of language from her favorite picture book for the first time.

"Will you read to me, Mommy?" I had said, climbing into her lap.

She took the storybook and smiled at my selection.

"Are you sure you wouldn't like to choose a different book today? We read *Too Many Kittens* yesterday."

"No, I like this one the best."

"All right, but today you'll help me read the words. Would you like that?"

I nodded eyes wide with enthusiasm. She had read the tale of the kittens and their adoptive homes many times, and, as she ran her finger beneath the words, I recited the story from memory, the groups of letters suddenly transforming into sound and meaning. When the last kitten found a home and my mother lifted her slender finger from the page, she closed the book and embraced me. I wrapped my thin arms around her neck, burying my face in her shoulder. I breathed in the familiar soothing scent of musk and cinnamon.

"You're growing up so fast," she had said, kissing my cheek."Soon you will read books all by yourself. It seems like only yesterday you were a baby."

"You read stories to me when I was in your tummy, didn't you, Mommy?" She had shared the memory with me many times before, but, as I often did, I asked the question anyway. I possessed a child's acute fascination with the events preceding my birth and with my arrival into the world.

"Yes, I have always read to you. I read to you while you lived in my tummy."

"Did I like it?"

"Yes, very much."

"How did you know?"

I fidgeted on her lap in anticipation of my favorite part of the account.

"You would wiggle and kick and move your tiny little elbows. That's when I knew you would always love books and stories, so I kept reading to you. I would put my hand on my belly and feel you dancing to the words. I knew you were happy."

"Then I was born and my feet came out first."

"Yes," she laughed."And you had a full head of black hair and the nurses put a pink bow in it."

"Was that a long time ago, Mommy? When I came out of your tummy? "

"Only four years."

"Is that a long time?"

Cradling my round cheeks in her hands, the wistfulness that only a mother can know swirled in her brown eyes. She shook her head."No, it's only the blink of an eye."

I blinked back the tears of longing that threatened escape from beneath my closed lids, my mind raw from the friction of time's rapid passage. Blindness had sifted through twenty years of learning and had deemed a mere handful of lessons useful, rending the majority of what I had come to know obsolete. Time looped back upon itself and hurled me, a reluctant and anxious woman of twenty-three, along with it. The regressive journey had flung me into moments better suited to an eager, bold child, and forced me to learn new lessons in walking, writing, and reading.

The unsteady secession of clicks registered from Carlos' slate blended with the dragging drone of my voice, creating a kind of dirge to mourn our accumulated losses. We had lost much more than just our eyesight. We had lost pieces of our identity. I no longer was a college student or a photographer. Carlos, after the arrival of the letter postmarked from Brazil, two typed pages which he could not read for himself, was no longer a husband. Perhaps in time the missing pieces would be replaced, but for now the hollow spaces remained empty as a starving belly, taunted by the memory of feasts once eaten and gnawed by the possibility that there might be no more.

Jane interrupted, halting our jerky rhythm."Excuse me for a moment, Amy. I'd like to look at Carlos' work before you finish."

Carlos swung the hinged slate open and slid the paper towards Jane. She scanned the page and handed it back to him.

"The first four lines look good, but the fifth and sixth lines are jumbled. You started in the wrong cell and wrote over top of what you had already written."

"Do you speak Portuguese, Jane?" Carlos asked, the grin he was trying to hide exposed in his tone.

"No."

"You don't? Well, in that case, let's just say that I wrote lines five and six in Portuguese."

Jane laughed and played along."Would you be so kind as to translate for us?"

Clearing his throat, Carlos launched into his per formative reading."Although I am the perfect man in so many ways," he began, his fingers pretending to produce words from the empty table top, "devilishly handsome, intellectually superior, and, of course, the world's greatest lover, I have but one flaw."

He paused for dramatic effect before he continued."There are chimpanzees who write Braille better than me and gorillas more skilled at reading it."

Jane and I applauded with mock bravado.

"You've done it, Carlos," I laughed."You've truly captured the experience. Couldn't have said it better myself."

The laughter felt good. I stretched my legs under the table, relaxing my back against the chair. Tension released its grip on my neck and I put my hands back on the book, prepared to take on the last four pages.

"What are you reading?" Carlos asked.

"Dick and Jane," I joked."Haven't you been paying attention? Doesn't my reading hold you spellbound? Let me catch you up to speed. When I left off, Dick was playing, Jane was smiling, and Spot was running."

"Seriously, I'm curious. It sounded like Faulkner. Is Jane making you read *A Rose for Emily*?"

"Yes."

"Do you make everyone read that story, Jane?" Carlos asked."I read it last week."

Jane smiled."Not everyone. Just you lucky students who I think are worthy. It's one of my favorites."

"You certainly have a dark side, Jane," Carlos said, and then turned my direction."Wait until you get to the end. You'll see what I mean. Perhaps we should all be a little leery of Miss Jane here."

"Yes, Carlos," Jane said, doing her best rendition of an elderly southern lady, "the old Braille spinster keeps some odd company after hours."

Carlos laughed and my curiosity spurred my fingers to the page, eager to share the inside joke. With the mood of the room lightened, my voice gained a hint of confidence and, although my pace had not quickened, the task seemed less tedious, less embarrassing, and less lonely. I crept through the final paragraphs, Carlos and Jane waiting in the wings for my reaction to the macabre tale. When I finished, I closed the book in stunned silence.

"Well," Jane said, as she took the volume and placed it on the shelf, "what do you think?"

"I'm impressed and repulsed. I loved it. Faulkner was a twisted genius," I said, filled with enthusiasm.

"So you like it as much as Jane does, don't you?" Carlos said, pushing his chair away from the table.

"Yes," I said again, "I loved it."

He stood and stepped towards the door."With that revelation, ladies, I'll leave you two scary women to your literary discussion."

Jane rose, slung her purse over a shoulder and grabbed her cane."I'm going to pick up some lunch at the little Greek place around the corner. Would you like to join me?"

I accepted Jane's invitation and we walked the two short blocks to the café. The rain slowed to a drizzle and tires hissed along the wet asphalt of Fifth Street. A steady stream of droplets ran from a canvas awning, tapping a syncopated beat on a soggy and forgotten bundle of Star Tribunes, the empty paper box standing, like a jilted lover, at the hotel's entrance. A hollow haunting gurgle echoed from the storm drains and businessmen's footsteps fell with muted splashes as they crept through the sidewalk's shallow puddles, trying to protect their Gucci loafers. Everywhere, the rain-soaked song of the city rendered its watercolor images, each sound a mental brush stroke in a portrait created for a blind eye.

Jane and I arrived at the Olympic Café and shook the rain from our coats. The restaurant was crowded and the owner yelled from behind the counter."Hey, ladies, there's an open spot to your right in the far corner."

"Thanks, Nico," Jane shouted over the hum of the noisy lunch crowd as we edged between the cramped tables.

Nico appeared a few minutes later, wiping his large hands on a white apron tied around his rotund waist."Can I interest you in the express lunch special?" he said, as he flipped to a blank page in his order pad."It's a gyro and a small salad."

Jane and I both took his suggestion and he penciled it in, adding our favorite extras.

"For you," he said to Jane, "extra feta on the salad." He turned towards me."And for this one, the one that looks just like my youngest girl, you want lots of olives."

I smiled at the pleasant proprietor. He never failed to mention my resemblance to his fifth daughter and he never forgot the preferences of his regular customers.

"How is she, your daughter?"I asked.

Nico beamed. He loved to brag about his children's accomplishments.

"This year, she'll graduate from law school," he said, his Mediterranean accented voice brimming with awe and pride."Can you believe it? One of my own, a lawyer. I am a blessed man to have five beautiful daughters."

I nodded in agreement. Nico hurried off to put in our order, his joy unexpectedly cracking a fragile shell, the shell never thick enough to shield my heart from the unresolved questions about my father's pride, his love, and his guilt. Was he proud of my refusal to break under the weight of my new dark world, or had his pride, along with his love, faded away like my eyesight? Did the emotional retreat I had felt from him since going blind stem from misplaced blame? Did he think I blamed him for the diabetes, for the blindness? Did he blame himself? When he looked in the mirror, when he looked at me, did he feel guilty for his fortunate recovery and for his relief in not having to share my fate? In the early hours of the morning, when my thoughts denied sleep, the questions stirred the stillness as I searched for answers among the utterances of my inner monologue, finding none.

My father and I rarely joined one another in the arena of sentimentality. Therefore, on Sunday afternoons, I tucked the questions safely away and dialed his number. He talked about the weather, the lawn, and his job at the factory. I talked about the weather, Minneapolis crime, and my classes at the rehab center. No tough questions asked. No tough answers given. No emotional risks taken.

Lunch arrived and I focused my attention on the food and on Jane's companionship.

"What happened in the hall this morning?" she asked."I caught the tail end of it."

"George called me a total."

"Really? That's low even for him. What did you say?"

"Nothing," I said, biting into the gyro.

"I bet you wanted to let him have it, didn't you?"

"No, not really. He's so pathetic and immature, I'm embarrassed for him. He spreads his hate around pretty evenly, so I can't take it too personally."

Jane unwrapped her utensils and laid the napkin on her lap."You're right about that. He told me that he didn't want to learn Braille from a blind woman. Said that a teacher should be able to see the students."

"He's got a huge chip on his shoulder, doesn't he? Does he think he's got it tougher than the rest of us?"

No," Jane said, her fork paused between the salad and her mouth, "I think George is trapped."

"Trapped?"

"Yes. He doesn't want to be blind, but he knows he's not sighted, so he stands in the middle, hating both sides equally because he can't seem to fit in with either one."

Although I had only spent a short time in the visual gray area of which Jane spoke, the memories of the confusion and frustration associated with it were fresh. George had been living there for eighteen years, never knowing release from its ambiguity.

Jane continued, "The irony of his insult about blind teachers is that when I was his age, I probably had the same amount of residual sight as he does, but half as much anger. The difference is I didn't kid myself."

She stabbed a chunk of feta cheese and an olive with her fork."I wasn't sighted. Never would be. The little bit of vision I did have only made me look clumsy when I tried too hard to rely on it. So I bought a cane, learned Braille, and threw away my pop bottle glasses."

"I can't imagine George making that decision. He likes to do things the hard way," I said, thinking of the violent outburst that had destroyed his sleep shades.

"Yes, he's not going to let go easily. He'll hold on as long as he can before he admits he's more blind than sighted," Jane agreed."But I guess we're all guilty of that sometimes, holding on when it would be healthier to accept the fact that wanting something doesn't necessarily make it ours."

The old spinster of Faulkner's story cast a shadow from her prison of delusion and isolation into the conversation.

"The Emily Complex."

She chuckled."I like that. You've just created a new syndrome people can claim to be suffering from."

We finished our lunch and hurried back to the center. The afternoon moved quickly and the early rush hour traffic began its slow noisy crawl outside the front door, a welcome sign that our day was almost done. As the last class ended, students mingled in the front lobby, making evening plans as they collected rain coats and bags for the bus ride home.

"Bernie and I are going to grab a beer at the Lion's Pub. Want to join us?" Paula asked, stopping beside my locker."I can take a look at that admissions form for you, if you like."

I slid the envelope marked with the University of Minnesota's seal from my bag."That would be great. I'd appreciate it. Is this it?"

She took it, inspecting the return address."Yes, that's it. My services will cost you though," she said, handing the envelope back.

"Name your price."

"Two beers."

"You work cheap." I smiled."I would've paid as much as three."

Carlos entered the lobby, engrossed in conversation with a young woman I didn't recognize, her warm pleasant laughter catching my ear.

"Who's that with Carlos?" I whispered to Paula.

"Her name's Molly. She's a potential student. I was swamped when she arrived for the tour, so I asked Carlos to do it."

"It sounds like he's doing an extremely charming job of it."

"You should see his face. I think she's the charming one. I've never seen Carlos smile quite that big."

I introduced myself to the attractive blond who, a year later, would become Carlos' wife. Not all of our lost identities remained lost. Carlos and Molly agreed to meet us at the pub and I followed Paula and Bernie out. The rain had stopped and patches of sunshine warmed the wet sidewalk. Noticing her husband's fatigue, Paula offered to push his wheelchair, but, as usual, Bernie declined. We reached the end of the block and, suddenly agitated with the sense that something was missing, I patted my empty pocket.

"Forgot my apartment keys. I'll catch up with you in a minute," I said, running back to the center to retrieve them.

George sat on the lobby sofa, engaged in a phone conversation. I tried not to listen, but his voice grew louder and whinier, making eavesdropping unavoidable.

"What do you mean you can't get me out of here? I told you before, I don't need training. I'm not blind!"

I rustled papers and jingled my keys as I grabbed them from the locker, shoving them into my purse. Thinking the disruptions would alert George to my close proximity, I cleared my throat, but he ignored the noises, not caring that I overheard his tirade.

"I hate this place and you can't force me to stay!" he screamed into the receiver, and then slammed it into the cradle.

I moved to the door and grasped the handle, not willing to serve as George's potential target again. But I hesitated, aware of the sniffling coming from the sofa.

"George," I said, reluctant to involve myself with his misery, but unable to ignore his obvious suffering, "Are you all right?"

Startled, he tried to regain composure, wiping his nose on his sleeve.

"I thought I was alone," he sniffed. "Uh…yeah, I'm okay. I just have some allergies, that's all."

I realized something more than just the fact he didn't admit to his tears. I realized the limitations of his sight. The "total" stood ten feet to his right and his eyes had failed to detect me. Sensing his embarrassment and knowing he had no intention of conversing further, I started to open the door, but let it close again. The unwanted image of the tall gangly teenager moping alone in the lobby invaded my thoughts although I tried to erase it. But George's acne scarred face would not leave, his sad eyes, magnified through thick lenses, telling tales of kickball games he was never asked to play and countless Friday nights without dates. They revealed all the birthday parties, the camping trips, and the Little League teams he missed. They spoke of bullies, cruel jokes, and humiliation.

"Some of us are meeting at the Lion's Pub on Sixth. Would you like to go?" I said.

A long silence followed. George, either too stunned by an invitation or too unfamiliar with social graces, messed with the straps on his backpack as if I had spoken to someone other than him.

My gesture placed him in a new and uncomfortable position. He could accept entrance into a circle of blind friends or he could remain alone, clinging to his hopes for admission into sighted society. We each waited at our separate thresholds.

"No," he finally said, his tone icy and distant, "I'm going back to the apartment. I'd rather be alone."

"Maybe next time, huh?" I said, offering another escape from his self-inflicted isolation.

"I doubt it," he said.

You and Emily, I thought, as I turned away from George and exited the rehabilitation center. *You and Emily.*

CHAPTER FIFTEEN

AUTUMN OF THE MONSTER AND THE SILVER BOX

"Raisins."

The word floated through the fog that enveloped my senses, barely audible, as if whispered from the opposite end of a far-reaching corridor. Confused, I could not recognize the voice, but the word, the sensation of cold bleached sheets pulled to my chin, the scent of antiseptic and alcohol, tugged at the loose threads of my memory. For a fleeting moment, I was the frightened child under the hospital bed again, peering at the dietician's battered loafers and hating her for suggesting to my mother that I should snack on the bitter dried fruits I disliked so much.

"Raisins," the voice repeated."They looked like shriveled grapes. Like raisins."

The heavy haze began to slowly lift and I tried to speak, aware that I wasn't the little girl under a hospital bed, but a grown woman lying on top of one. Although the question of "when" had been resolved, the "where" and "why" swam around in the murky waters of my mind. Regardless of the answers, no one would convince me I should eat any damn raisins. Of that, I was sure. I hated them then. I hated them now.

But for all my indignation, my parched lips managed only to produce a pitiful moan. A latex gloved hand patted my shoulder.

"Welcome back. Your surgery went well."

The final layer of anesthesia fog lifted, jarred me into reality, and all of the missing pieces slid into place. The voice didn't belong to my nemesis, the dietician. It belonged to Dr. Marjorie Rubinstein, a reconstructive ophthalmological surgeon. The raisins of which she referred weren't the petrified rabbit turd variety one found in the snack-size box, either. They were my infected, atrophied eyes.

"We successfully removed them. It took a little longer than the three hours I estimated."

"How long?" I said in a hoarse whisper.

Another hand grasped mine and squeezed tightly. "Five hours," Mom said, then released my hand to brush the hair from my forehead.

"There was a great deal of scar tissue and it took some very intricate cutting to salvage the muscle," Dr. Rubinstein explained."But we did it and the orbs are implanted, so you will have movement when it is healed and you are fitted with the sclera shells."

After I lost my sight and began rehabilitation training, I had thought that ophthalmologist visits, procedures, and miserable recovery periods had ended. But as the sultry days of summer gave way to the brisk Minnesota autumn, a situation arose that would not be ignored. My eyes grew irritated and red, the burning sensation increasing until I no longer could stand even the weight of the air on their raw surface. Determined to push on with my training, I moved through my assigned lessons, eyelids closed, until at last I lost the ability to open them. The condition persisted and I applied bottle after bottle of prescription drops, ointments, and lubricants prescribed by well-meaning ophthalmologists. Nothing worked

"Have you thought about having your eyes removed?" Alicia, a fellow diabetic rehab student had asked over coffee one morning as I splashed yet another useless dose of medication onto my discolored iris.

"No way!" I said, doing little to hide my mortification."I'm done with that kind of butchery."

"It may sound like a pretty extreme approach, but I had one of mine removed a few years ago and I'm glad I did. The damn thing was infected and it hurt all the time. Kept me awake at night and it got to the point where I couldn't stand to open it. I went around like I was winking at everyone."

She laughed at the recollection and I grew irritated, suddenly perceiving Alicia's humor as callous and cold. Perhaps she had developed the ability to create comedy from her diabetic complications, but I still struggled, vacillating between my admiration for her positivism and the worry that the blind double amputee with the failing kidneys and numb fingers was a crystal ball's image of my own future.

Realizing that I had not joined her in the personal joke, she stopped laughing and slid an arm around my shoulder."Listen, honey. I don't mean to be so hard core. I know this is difficult stuff to hear, but I've got twenty years on you and a lot of experience with the ways diabetes can cause you to hurt. If I didn't laugh sometimes, I'd probably start crying and never stop."

I laid my hand over hers and hoped that the neuropathy-numbed fingers could still translate the love in my touch.

"I'll give you the name of an ophthalmologist I think can help you. Dr. Rubinstein is a straight shooter. Please, go see her. Infection is nothing for a diabetic to mess around with, especially that close to the brain."

Alicia's voice caught for a moment, emotion threatening."Diabetes is cruel. It robs us of our legs. Sometimes it steals our kidneys. And if sight wasn't enough, sometimes it even wants our eyes. But if that's the price the monster has set for you, Amy, pay it. Don't wait so long that the price goes up. What it collects will be too dear, too precious a price to pay."

With a prescription for morphine in my pocket and my mother and Dennis supporting each of my arms, I stepped into the gray November afternoon as a bitter north wind slapped our faces. The insurance provider did not deem the bilateral enucleation of one's eyes worthy of a hospital stay, and as we crossed the deserted street in front of the Phillips Eye Institute, returning to the ramp where we had left the car that morning, I was actually relieved. I would spend the approaching Thanksgiving holiday with my family, healing with the help of medicine that only home can provide. I slept, wrapped in a blanket, as Dennis sped south on I35, the IDS Tower shrinking along with the rest of the Minneapolis skyline in the rear window. Dreams of pumpkin pie, Grandmother Tott's beautiful snow-white hair, and the sound of Grandpa Lynn's singing *House of the Rising Sun* rocked me in my unconscious cradle; I wore the peaceful mask of ignorance, the blissful unawareness of the days that lay ahead, my imagination's failure to conjure the terror I would find there.

The man in the tailored black suit stood at the foot of my bed. His black eyes locked with mine in an uninterrupted oily stare, his thin lipless mouth curled at the corners. His hair, slicked back from his unnaturally smooth forehead, appeared almost blue in its blackness against the milky pallor of his skin. A blood-red tie lay neatly knotted against a starched white shirt. As he casually began to withdraw his concealed hand from the jacket's pocket, I caught the gaudy glimmer of the diamond cufflink that adorned the crisp snowy fabric. Everything in his demeanor, everything in his appearance was disturbingly ordinary, yet the threat of his presence hung in the room like the foul odor of something rotting, something dead. My flesh crawled and, terrified, I threw the comforter off, raising my arms to protect myself.

"I see you!" I screamed."I know who you are!"

He didn't reply, the grin still frozen on his waxen face, as he drew his hand the rest of the way from the pocket. It was balled and either held something he wished to reveal or else he was preparing to strike a blow. As he unfolded his fist, both possibilities became reality. At the end of each pale finger a dagger-like nail jutted, grotesque in their long length, yet precisely manicured. The ends were filed into five perfect points, created with the intent to inflict great destruction.

"Stay the fuck away from me!"I flailed my arms, frantically punching the air.

The monster, manifested from the mixture of my surgical mutilation and morphine, laughed, enjoying my terror."You're afraid?" he said, feigning dejection."After all of the years you and I have known one another?"

Levitating, rather than stepping, onto the bed, he crouched like a gargoyle. His bare feet resembled his hands, the nails more like the claws of an animal, and he clenched his toes around the edge of the mattress like some prehistoric winged creature tearing its talons into the broad back of its prey. I kicked my legs, my arms still attacking the empty space around me, dumb to the notion that I couldn't harm a hallucination.

"Don't you want to see what I keep in my pocket?" he asked, extending his open palm."You did say you can see, didn't you?"

No longer fixated on the hideous fingernails that had initially held my attention, I saw what lay in the monster's hand. He held a pair of shiny blue eyes, their pupils aimed at my colorless face. Though they weren't the raisin-like mutations Dr Rubinstein had removed, I recognized them.

"Yours?"

I nodded and reached for them, delusional enough in my terror and distress to believe the monster had offered a second chance. With the Cheshire grin of a politician who has just won the election based on promises he never intended to keep, my adversary snatched the fragile treasure away, and dug the pointy nails into the moist tissue with sadistic glee before depositing the punctured eyes back into the depths of his musty pocket.

"Mine!" he said, rising to his full height and looming victoriously above me.

He spread his arms wide as if he might launch himself from the bed, sail down the hall way, and take flight into the moonless sky, but he lingered, savoring my misery."It's all mine: the legs, the kidneys, the heart, the uterus. Mine, mine, mine!"

His hot, sickeningly sweet breath brushed my face and shrieks exploded from me, every cell of my body lending its power to the primal screams.

The door burst open and I felt firm but gentle hands restrain my flailing wrists as someone urged my rigid body back against the sweat-soaked sheets.

"I saw him! I saw that mother fucker! He was right here!" I ranted, fighting to sit up again."I can see, damn it! Don't you hear me? I can see!"

Dennis pulled the comforter to my neck, tucked the sides securely under the mattress, and my mother crawled onto the bed, strapping her arm across my writhing chest. Exertion endangered the tender tissue of my eye sockets and her voice grew louder in my ear with every jerk and twist of my head.

"Stop thrashing! You're safe. There's no one here but Dennis and me."

As the effects of the morphine dwindled and sensation began to reclaim the raw swollen layers hidden behind the plastic conformers and sutured eyelids, I retreated in an exhausted heap. Soon the next round of proliferating pain would begin: every tooth in my mouth aching as if abscessed, the sensation of shattered cheek bones, the freshly cut eye muscles pinched by a pair of invisible pliers, the hatchet lodged in my forehead, the burning sinus cavities, and the feeling that the bridge of my nose had smashed into a brick wall. The small window of relief had opened, offering a temporary safe haven between agony so intense it brought me to my knees, vomiting until I blacked out, and the hallucinogenic realm where the monster waited, his pockets alive with more of the skittering insects I felt racing over my flesh. I slept until the window slammed shut and I took the morphine tablet from my mother as Dennis handed me a glass of water to wash it down.

Choosing terror over agony seemed like no choice at all and I grasped for something sane to hold on to as I began another gradual liquid journey to the distorted destinations of the narcotic.

"I'm going to sit at the table with everyone else on Thanksgiving," I said, my voice raspy from screaming. "I'll get up and get dressed. I'll have some turkey and some of Grandma's pumpkin pie. Just like a real person."

Dennis sat the glass on the night table and Mom clicked off the lamp.

"You'll see. Thanksgiving dinner with real people, just like a real person, because that's what I am."

I began to slide down the slippery tunnel and the words faded until I was the only one that could comprehend their meaning. "I'm not an eyeless freak. I'm real."

Two days later, I emerged from the bedroom as I said I would. The aroma of roasted turkey and herb stuffing filled the duplex. Dennis arranged logs and kindling in the fireplace, and the soothing sound of familiar voices engaged in conversation resonated from the living room and kitchen. I shuffled around the corner from the hallway, a haggard prizefighter in an old bathrobe, belt untied, and a pair of stained sweat shorts with an over-sized T-shirt. I knew that deep shades of purple ringed both of my bruised sockets; their sunken hollow appearance made it impossible to ignore the missing eyeballs.

There was a pause, just long enough for everyone's shock at my appearance to register, but not long enough to hurt my feelings with their silence. Heidi stood and offered me the chair next to the rocker where my great grandmother sat. Mary helped guide me to it. Dennis' youngest daughters had arrived the day before and, after deciding that their fear for me was greater than their fear of me, took turns holding my hand as I wrestled with my morphine foe, oblivious of the young girls' committed bedside vigil.

"We're glad you could join us," Grandmother Tott said, her matriarchal tone the cue for conversation to resume.

Though her fingers were crooked with age, I could tell by her touch that she wore the massive rings of silver and precious stones, and I thought of our disappearing stars as she cupped my face in her hand, the sparkling gems cool against my cheek.

"I'm glad to be here."

Dennis tousled my messy hair in recognition of my kept promise. The autumn chill still clung to his hand from a recent trip to the wood pile. I tried to calculate the days since I had felt the fresh air on my skin. The logs crackled and popped in the fireplace as the buzz of an electric knife signaled that turkey carving was underway.

Dennis ducked into the kitchen, returned with a sample slice, and gave me half."That's a fetching outfit you're wearing," he said.

I smiled weakly, the expression feeling odd after being absent for so long, and remembered what Alicia had said about laughter versus tears.

"Like it?" I said, stretching my leg out under the terrycloth robe's hem."It's kind of a fusion of disgruntled housewife meets asylum patient meets foxy boxer."

"Classy. Don't let your mom see it, though. She'll want to run right out and buy one just like it."

Mother walked from the kitchen as she wiped gravy off her fingers with a dish towel."Are you teasing her?" she said, glaring at Dennis as if he were the bully who had blackened my eyes."She looks fine. She looks beautiful. Don't tease her!"

She grabbed my hands in hers and I could feel them tremble, her emotions too delicate, too strained.

"It's all right, Mom."

"No, it's not," she said, shaking her head and dropping my hands into my lap as she hurried to exit the room before the tears fell.

Don't start, I thought as the bathroom door closed behind her, or you will never stop.

Some wounds heal slowly: the ones cut into a mother's heart, the ones shaped by a child's woes, formed by her child's loss. Time and the salt of her tears provide the only soothing medicine. Many seasons passed, many autumns, until, again, my mother and I walked together through the fallen leaves, at last discovering the healing place.

Carrying the bushel basket between us, we crossed the wide lawn, through the grove of trees, to the vegetable garden. When we reached the edge, I laid my white cane in the grass and followed my mother through the pumpkin, squash, and cucumber vines. I pulled a pair of borrowed work gloves from the pocket of my overalls and squatted among the plants, searching among the tangled foliage for the vegetables to harvest.

"Just leave the rotted ones. I'll gather them later for the compost box," my mother said."Nothing goes to waste."

The seeds she had so lovingly planted in the earth that spring and, throughout the summer, tended with care, had come to fruition. Dozens of fat zucchini squash lay hidden in the twisted green leaves, ripe for grinding and making bread. She had already lined the pantry shelves with jars of home-canned tomatoes for the approaching winter. The blue jays circled the droopy yellow sunflowers, collecting nourishment from the broad black centers as they cried their shrill appreciation to the gardener who planted seeds just for them.

My mother had moved to an acreage, away from the city, away from the memories, and, in the spring of their arrival to the country, Dennis had tilled a plot. She returned to the garden, where she had always found peace in the softness of the earth and promise in the warmth of the sun. She whispered her prayers for healing, for growth; the garden grew lush and healthy. But kneeling now, in the midst of another bountiful harvest, she cried as she stared at my eyes. Painted, polished plastic, so realistic in their color, in their motion, most people did not know they weren't the originals. But she knew. And when she looked at them, memory squeezed her heart in its fist. The prostheses' beauty could not obliterate the ugliness of the silver box.

"I saw them," she said."I couldn't tell you then, but I did see them."

I paused, sitting back on my haunches as I tossed an over-ripe cucumber in the direction of the compost pile.

"Saw what?"

"Your eyes. I saw your eyes the day Dr. Rubinstein removed them."

"What do you mean?"

"After your surgery, before they let me come back to the post op, I was sitting in the waiting area. I was alone. Dennis had gone for coffee and the lounge was empty."

She moved closer."A man came in the side entrance, carrying a box with some labels on the side. I didn't pay much attention until he turned into the hall where the surgical suites were. I suddenly knew what he was there for and I had a moment where I couldn't catch my breath."

With the corneas too damaged for transplantation, I had requested that my eyes be donated for scientific research. I told Dr. Rubinstein I hoped they would provide knowledge about diabetic retinopathy, but my darker ulterior motive was to wave the failure of medical science in the faces of its practitioners.

"I stared at the hallway. I was afraid to even blink. I had to see that silver box. Had to see him carry it out and leave with it so it would be real to me. Does that make any sense?"

I nodded.

"When he came out, I locked my eyes on that box. I knew what was inside and I kept focused on the damn thing as he carried it all the way to the door. I wanted to do something, say something, but I didn't know what. Then, as he started to push the door open, I said the only thing I could think of in the moment. I said 'good-bye'. It was all I could do."

She inhaled, the out breath, a long sob. "I felt so damn helpless. Like everything I've ever done to protect you was a joke. Some stranger carried my daughter's eyes away in a box, a box with a 'Biological Waste Material' label on it, and all I could do was stare."

I grasped my mother's shoulders faced her, and forced her to look into the only eyes afforded me by fate."It's not your fault. The diabetes, the blindness, the surgeries. None of it is your fault."

"But what if it is my fault? What if your blindness is a punishment? My punishment for being a bad mother, a bad person."

My cheeks flushed and I clenched my teeth as I recalled a potential source of her guilt. Shortly after losing my sight, one of the concerned Christian ladies of the community had suggested that sin was at the root of my affliction. When my mother rose to my defense, the woman countered by pointing an accusing finger at her.

"Perhaps God is punishing you through your daughter's suffering. After all, you did commit adultery."

I wondered if cruelty based in a false sense of moral superiority carried an equally stiff divine penalty, suddenly consumed with the desire to lift the heavy brick of shame off my mother's conscience and smash her accuser in the head with it. The wind shifted and a low-flying flock of Canadian geese appeared above the grove. I closed my eyes and let my aggravation wane, as I listened to the flapping wings.

"Do you remember the butterflies last fall?" I asked.

"Yes," my mother said, brightening at the thought of the incredible sight.

Thousands of monarchs, weary in their southern migration, had landed in the trees beside the garden. In the early September sunset, the branches blazed with the brilliant orange and black insects. Mother and I had stood beneath the trees, our faces turned towards the sea of fluttering fragile wings.

"You looked at them as if you were seeing them," she said."Your face was tilted up towards all that beauty your eyes couldn't see and it made me want to scream. I wanted to scream to God or the world or whoever would listen. It's so damn unfair!"

I took her hand. "Do you remember the wonderful sound? The soft rustling hum, like energy?"

"No"

"I do."   I kissed her cheek."I'll always remember that sound of butterflies in the trees. I don't think that's unfair. I don't think it's a punishment, do you?"

"No, it's a blessing," she said, wiping her eyes.

"It's not as dark in here as you may think."

As the sun sank behind the barn's cupola, we departed the healing garden and left behind what we could not use. Among the rotted squash and dieing vines, the monster sat and searched his pockets for what was no longer there. He opened the silver box beside him, but found it empty, too. Carrying the basket full of vegetables, my mother and I passed beneath the trees, the color of monarch's in our minds' eye, the hum of their wings singing in our ears.

CHAPTER SIXTEEN

WINTER OF THE SNAKE

The students poured out the classroom's rear doors and I stepped into the flow of people filing up the aisle, canvas book bag slung over my shoulder, white cane in my hand. The snow had started again and, as I left Scott Hall, the feathery flakes clung to my eyelashes, their silent descent peaceful and dreamy. I hesitated at the top of the stairs, enjoying the sensation, but nervously aware of how slippery the sidewalk would be with another wet layer accumulating on the already icy pavement. Peeling off a glove, I felt for the watch on my wrist and flipped the glass open. The hand's position against the raised metal dots on the face only added to my anxiety and I hurried down the slick steps, hoping I wouldn't break my neck in the rush. Piles of snow lined the curb; raking my cane along the top, I judged the obstacle to be about chest high. With an exasperated sigh, I climbed the frozen heap. Like a blind defender in a game of King on the Mountain, I perched at the top, leaned on my cane, and waited for the cars, their roofs level with my boots, to pass. Someone shouted at me.

"Hey, lady! Be careful. It's scooped out down here at the corner."

I smiled at the concerned citizen and, noticing that the traffic had cleared, gave a thumbs up before sliding down the opposite side and crossing the street.

The shortest distance between any two points..., I thought, remembering the old rule and successfully scaling the snow bank on the other side.

The University of Minnesota campus provided geographical challenges: the Mississippi cutting it into two sections, the roads and walkways a jumble of twists, turns, and dead ends. I had soon discovered the advantage of figuring out buildings and locations in relationship to one another. Knowing that Nickelson, the building that housed the Disabled Student Service Office, stood almost straight across Pleasant Street from Scott Hall shaved minutes off when I was running late and, like most college students, oblivious to jaywalking laws.

The receptionist greeted me as I stepped into the cramped office, flushed and breathless.

"You have a stack of tapes. One of the readers just dropped them off," she said.

Running my fingers along the shelf reserved for audio cassettes, I found the Braille label marked with my name and deposited the tapes into my book bag. Although many of my college texts were available through professional recording services for the disabled or through the state's library for the blind, DSS took up the slack. The readers mostly consisted of work study recipients, who managed to include a lot of yawning and gum-chewing along with the audio material. But despite all of the mispronounced words and frequent giggling, they provided an invaluable service for visually impaired and dyslexic students.

"Does Daniel Levin have any tapes?" I asked, searching for the correct label.

"Doesn't look like it. One of our usual called in sick today. Bet he won't have any until tomorrow."

With a midterm to study for and no taped text available, he would have to spend valuable time searching for someone to read the chapters out loud. Daniel would be pissed; I didn't look forward to being the bearer of the bad news. As I left the office, I mentally filed through my list of alternate readers, hoping that Mandy would be available. I had lucked out and spotted her name on a volunteer list my first semester. Enrolled in an art history course, a seemingly masochistic choice for a blind student, I called her for an interview.

"So you want me to record descriptions of the art photographed in this book?" she had asked, thumbing through the hundreds of glossy pages. "I haven't ever done something like this. I usually just read text, but I'll do my best."

After listening to the first few minutes of Mandy's pleasing voice sculpt an Assyrian relief, I knew I had discovered a treasure. I aced the course, much to the surprise of the skeptical professor who had "strongly encouraged" my withdrawal, and much to the delight of Mandy, reader extraordinaire. At that point, I had offered her a raise, but she had refused more money, instead providing transportation to the grocery store twice a month and assisting me with mail. She said that dollars couldn't be deposited in the "Bank of Karma," her kindness creating the balance in my otherwise frustrating first year back at college.

The air, thick with snow, stung my cheeks and I pulled the scarf around my nose and mouth against the wind bearing down on the mall pedestrians like an icy freight train as I passed Northrop Auditorium. Following the route Daniel taught me during my initial terrifying days as a blind student, I avoided the benches, waste cans, and clusters of coeds. Winter vacated the sidewalks of a white cane user's greatest enemies, bicycles and roller blades, and a bit of tension lifted with their absence. Hobbling home with a broken cane stub tended to ruin a good mood in a hurry. But I would have several more frigid months before the speeding wheels returned to the trail, the trail where, that autumn, Daniel and I had encountered the mountain bike rider.

"Shit! Watch where you're going," The guy had yelled, jumping off his Mongoose to check it for damage.

I stood, speechless, the sound of the sickening crack still ringing in my ears.

"Dan, my cane," I finally managed, as I touched the splintered end and brushed my foot over the sidewalk in search of the six inches of missing fiberglass that had lodged in the bicycle's spokes.

The guy yanked the fragment of cane from the wheel."What the hell is this?"

"Are you serious?" Daniel said through clenched teeth as he moved closer to me.

I held out my hand and the bicyclist gave me the piece.

"It's the end of my cane," I said, then reached for Daniel's arm in hopes of defusing his irritation, which I could tell mounted with each new word the cyclist uttered.

Shoving the broken end into my bag, my own emotions flared. It had been my first cane, the one Daniel and Mitchell had given me at our introduction. The bicycling genius stared, the concept bouncing off his brain like a pebble off of the neon safety helmet my imagination had placed on his head.

"Cane?" he said.

"Yes, asshole, it's a cane," Daniel said. "My girlfriend's blind and you just broke her fucking cane. What are you going to do about it?"

"Oh, dude, that sucks!" he said dismissively."You're screwed!" Jumping back on his cane killer, he had peddled away from the scene of the crime, leaving Daniel, red-faced, in the middle of the sidewalk. I grabbed his elbow, grateful his cane hadn't become a casualty, too, but he pulled away to swear at the departing bicyclist. I had started to protest, but stopped, sensing that the helplessness he felt, the helplessness of a blind man in a world of sighted men, far exceeded the aggravation of my mobility dilemma. When he had calmed, I tried again, taking his sleeve.

"I can't do this without you,"

"Like *I'm* any damn help to you!"

"You're the only one with a cane and I would like to get home before dark, so I guess I would consider you helpful."

"You know what I mean. That two-wheeled prick just mangled your cane. I should have punched him in his smug mouth!"

I rolled my eyes. The macho crap always bored me and, although I would have liked to have taken a swing at the guy myself, what I wanted more was to put the whole disturbing incident behind us and go home.

"Dan," I said," haven't you heard? Chivalry is dead, but I can't get to the bus stop without your help, so if you want to revive it, the best thing to do is to start by giving me your damn arm."

He blew out an exasperated breath. He was still ticked off, but unable to argue the practicality of my point. I took his elbow and he swayed to the left, pressing my shoulder with his weight. Caught off guard by the unexpected movement, I stumbled, then, alarmed that we might both hit the concrete and crack something more serious than a fiberglass cane, I straightened and slid an arm around his waist to steady him.

"Sugar?" I asked, already unzipping my bag and rifling through the jumble of slates, note books, and cassette tapes before he could answer.

Cans of soda were the most convenient item to carry for such emergencies and I popped open the Coke and handed it to Daniel.

"Thanks," he said, downing half the can in two long swallows."I had to drink mine during communications lecture."

As a couple sped passed on roller blades, we stepped off the sidewalk and sat down in the grass. I touched Daniel's arm, noticing the perspiration on his skin.

"Are you angry or is this low blood sugar?"

He rubbed his sweaty forearm. "Both," he said.

Had it not been for the shakiness of Dan's hand as he clutched the can of life-saving liquid and the ruined hunk of useless white fiberglass jutting from my bag, we might have been the students pictured on the cover of the admissions brochure. But, despite his colorful rugby jersey and my All-American ponytail, life never delegated roles as normal as that to people like us. We both knew it; Daniel often caring too much and me, perhaps, not caring enough. The wheels had just kept buzzing through the fallen oak leaves, their hum a reminder of our social relegation.

Consigned to a subterranean corner of the medical complex, the dialysis unit was a cinderblock cavern of florescent lights and quietly humming machines that loomed behind a half dozen recliners. When I arrived ten minutes late, most of the chairs were occupied, but as I shook the melting snow from my hair and pulled off my gloves, prepared to do what I did for four hours three days a week, the nurse approached.

"Dan's not here," he said."Go ahead and take a load off."

"Where is he? I thought he had an appointment today."

He does, but there was a problem with his line and the on-call doc is on her way down to replace it."

I swung the padded stool I usually used from under a table as he adjusted the settings on the machine and scratched a notation on a clipboard.

"It may be a while before Dan gets back and we get him hooked up. I'd grab the recliner if I were you."

"No thanks," I said, throwing my coat over the chair's armrest.

The movie *Steel Magnolias* trickled into memory like the icy droplets of melted snow still dripping down my bare neck.

The young diabetic mother bends to lift her son. They named him Jack Jr., after his father. But she suddenly clutches her lower back, tumbling to the floor, kidneys failing, her child bawling for the attention she cannot give him. Despite the scene's dramatization, for the reality of nephropathy was far uglier, it kept me frozen to the spot on the tiny wheeled stool.

No, I thought, that's not my chair, not yet.

An hour passed, but Dan hadn't returned. Trying to utilize the time wisely, I reviewed pages of lecture notes, but lacked the concentration needed to commit any of it to memory. The woman in the recliner adjacent to Dan's woke from the nap she had been taking since my arrival and flipped on the mini television attached to her chair. She cranked the volume, the distorted tinny echo of a McDonald's ad driving me to shove the wrinkled Braille paper back into my book bag and my stomach to rumble with hunger. The pot of chili in our refrigerator, a hot bubble bath, and my flannel pajamas called, but it would be several hours until I could answer. The lower muscles of my back ached and I propped my feet on the reclining Naugahyde nightmare. The man-made fabric always seemed to upholster many of the less luxurious, more monotonous locales: the dentist's chair with the head rest that always pinched at the neck; the exam table of the gynecologist, its unwelcoming surface hidden under even more unwelcoming crisp white paper; over-booked doctor's waiting rooms where the kids coughed without covering their mouths and the only reading material available was pamphlets detailing different types of cancer. Anywhere people did not really want to be, but usually were forced to burn up far too many of life's valuable minutes, it appeared. If purgatory really existed, it was probably filled with obnoxious orange recliners just like the one under my feet.

The nurse stopped across the aisle, examined the intravenous line in the woman's arm, and frowned at what he saw.

"Looks like we have a collapsed vein here, Mrs. Metzger."

"Again? This happened Monday, too," she said as she turned the sound down on the television and pulled herself up in the chair.

"Your veins haven't been very cooperative this week. We may need to set you up for a CVTC."

The CVTC, short for Central Venous Tunneled Catheter, was a device which, when inserted into an incision below the collar bone, threaded into the patient's Superior Vena Cava and acted as a semi-permanent line. Dan had worn one since he began dialysis that autumn in preparation for transplantation, his mother a match and willing donor. Without a living candidate and with long waiting lists for cadaver organs, the ten inches of exposed rubber tubing had been taped to my father's chest for nearly a year. Regardless of the stellar attitude I had developed towards procedures and the apparatus involved, neither personal experience nor exposure had steeled me against the almost phobic horror and repulsion I had for the Hickman catheters. When I hugged my father, I flinched at the disconcerting coil concealed under his shirt. Dan could not see the sickened expression upon my face the first time my fingers inadvertently brushed the hump of flesh saddling the serpentine shunt, the way I grew pale when he asked for help cleaning the area with antiseptic swabs, or how I shivered every time the nurse joined the double ends to their mates and the dialysis machine pumped the poisons from his blood.

Crossing my arms over my chest, I clutched my shoulders, my palms pressed against my collar bones. How much longer did I have before diabetes would mandate that I, too, should carry the serpent-like extension beneath my blouse? A sudden surge of intense urgency shot through me and I sat up on the stool, wanting to escape, *needing* to escape the incessant hum of the machines, the rows of Naugahyde recliners, the pungent smell of rubbing alcohol and faint coppery odor of blood. I wanted to rush through the double doors and run until I was safe from the snake that raised from Daniel's chest, the monster destroying Daniel's kidneys, the reflection of myself in the mirror that Daniel's life had created. But any plans of acting upon my intense desire to flee were squelched by Daniel's voice in the corridor.

"I didn't think you'd still be here. Aren't you sick of waiting? "

I moved my coat off of the recliner, feeling guilty and angry at my anxiety, my weakness, and my disloyalty. He sat down and propped his feet up. The nurse arrived and linked Daniel's Hickman to the machine.

"Did you stop at DSS?" he asked."I called them after you left for class and they told me my tapes aren't ready."

"Yes, I stopped there. Sorry about that. I'll call Mandy when we get home."

"Thanks, but I made arrangements. I lined up a guy from the class who says he hasn't read the material yet himself so he'll meet me at the union tomorrow morning. He'll do it for breakfast and coffee."

I admired his ability to pull yet another trick from his sleeve; a skill which, for a man juggling diabetes, blindness, kidney disease, and college simultaneously, was a necessity. Charisma was Dan's trump card and few could resist the magnetism of his wit and conviviality; his inability to see never detracting from his ability to be seen.

As the nurse completed his tasks, he handed Dan the call button.

"Should I use this if I need you to bring me a cheeseburger?"

"Well, maybe if you need a beer or a lap dance," the nurse laughed, pulling the curtain and blocking the view of the neighboring recliner, "but the doctors frown upon us serving up red meat to our kidney patients."

Dan's jovial mood exited along with the nurse and we sat in uncomfortable silence for several minutes before he took my hand and squeezed it tightly. His cold clammy touch disturbed me and I fought the already present urge to pull away from the grip that felt more like control than affection. His voice was disconcerting and hollow.

"That was fucking horrible," he said.

I winced, the turquoise rings cutting into the sides of my fingers as his hold strengthened. Did he know how much I wanted to run? How if he had returned to the dialysis unit a few minutes later than he had, I would have been gone? My fingers tingled and I wiggled them a little, hoping that he would release them, but he didn't.

"The catheter had slipped and it had to be adjusted so the blood could flow. They kept working the God damn thing in and out, an inch at a time, until I thought I was gonna fucking scream."

The discomfort in my hand shifted to the pit of my gut.

"I could feel everything," he continued, the rising anger drowning out any apprehensiveness, "deep in my chest, in my heart. It was like something crawling, wiggling. I thought I was going to lose it. My heart kept racing and I just gripped the table and clenched my teeth until the fluttering stopped."

I fought the sickening sensation that had invaded my own chest, the rapid fire twitch of pulse that seemed to mimic Dan's description and I laid my free hand on top of his, not sure which one of us my gesture was truly intended to console. He eased his grip and my fingers awoke with a throb. Behind him, Dan's temporary mechanical kidney clicked quietly into another medically miraculous sequence of functions and the charming young man with whom I shared a bed, blindness, and a son-of-a-bitch of a disease, emerged.

"You better watch out. The on-call doctor was pretty cute and she was hitting on me. Told me I had nice dark curly hair."

"Really? That's very interesting," I said, exaggerating the tinge of jealousy I once would have felt, but no longer could detect on the emotional radar."Are you and the hot doctor meeting for dinner after this?"

"No, of course not. Oh, sure, she made my heart do back flips, but I think she cheated; using that catheter trick on a guy doesn't count. You, on the other hand, only had to say my name and I was a goner."

I looked away, absently forgetting for a moment that he could not see my face, his words trussing me with more force than his hand. There might have been a time in the not so distant past when they would have been welcome, bringing a blush to my cheeks, making me smile at the sentiment, but much had changed and I no longer derived the same pleasure from his tenderness. So much of what had initially drawn me to Daniel had transformed, and had become the reason for my ever-increasing desire to separate from him.

Knowing that he had lived for as many years as I had with the monster that had robbed us of our sight, being the recipient of empathy rather than sympathy, and struggling beside someone who understood the daily frustrations, the duality of our experiences in life seemed to create a well-matched pair. But the transformation had arrived with the snake coiled just above Dan's collar bone and, like the one that had shown up on the edge of a dusty gravel road long before Daniel's heart had been invaded by either the pretty doctor's catheter or the sound of my voice, its arrival heralded a forthcoming and unfavorable ending.

**

Hot wind blew through the open windows and great gritty clouds billowed from the truck's tires as we sped along the sun-baked road towards the lone tree. It had been JD's idea to visit and Nora and I had agreed, she eager to shoot more photos and I needing to take in its strength with eyes that were quickly failing. Susanna, a newcomer to our ritual, pointed through the dirty windshield at the hill.

"Is that it? Up there?"

The spectral bare branches stretched upward like emaciated hands beckoning for a final drink from the sky's liquid blueness and I shivered despite the summer heat. Had I not come for my final drink, as well?

"Yes, that's it," I said, wondering what Susanna thought of the old tree that JD, Nora, and I had returned to time and again.

She squinted, bending to see under the cracked visor as the truck crested the hill, and then slowed.

"It's just like you described it," she said, smiling knowingly, never glancing away.

I had shared the tree's description with her our first night as college roommates. We had lounged on the shabby carpeting of our unfurnished apartment as we finished off a bottle of wine and recounted our childhood stories. She had an appreciation for the one-tree hill, having grown up in one of the other small rural towns that dotted the Iowa map. Each community possessed that grassy river bank, icy gravel pit swimming hole, or rutted back woods dirt path that had a magical appeal for its teenage residents. It was the place where you might drink your first keg beer or park with your steady guy after a Friday night football game. It was a place where you hung out with friends, making big plans and talking big dreams or, on lonelier afternoons, go to cry over lost love, lost hopes, lost innocence. But no matter how far your journey and the years took you from the nostalgic location, you remembered the vibrant feeling of youth attached to it and it was always part of your homecoming.

The west end of Silver Lake where the solitary tree stood was that kind of place and Susanna paid it homage as any good small-town girl would, jumping out of the truck cab as JD stopped in the field inlet. She crawled over the rock pile to get a closer look at the gnarled old trunk, and Nora slid out behind her, snapping Susanna's picture. JD, more than a little smitten with the bubbly blond, posed next to her, an arm wrapped casually around her shoulder.

"Take another one," he urged as Nora advanced the film in her Nikon.

A crow sat on a fence post and watched with shiny obsidian eyes. It cawed at the odd impromptu photo shoot. Leaning against the front bumper, I admired the ancient tree, my eyes watering behind dark sun glasses from the bright afternoon glare, but although the recent laser treatments had increased the sensitivity and irritation, I willed myself not to blink. For in an instant of inexplicable panic, I knew that if I shut my lids, even for a second, it all would disappear: the haughty crow, the jagged pile of rocks, the dust-coated Ford, the shimmering lake beyond, JD, Nora, Susanna, the tree. Everything would be gone. All would still exist, but not in my world. I stared until the wind carried the bone-dry powder from the surface of the gravel road. It stung my eyes and forced me to shut them. I silently cursed the paralyzing possibility that would, in another season, become truth.

JD ambled over, sat on the bumper, and crossed his long legs at the ankle.

"Man, I've really missed days like this. Just cruisin' with you and Nora. Listening to tunes, havin' a few beers. Since you went to college and Nora moved to Milwaukee, I hardly get to see you guys. I miss that."

"I've missed it, too. This has been a great day, the kind we can think about when summer is over and really smile. Kind of a last hurrah. A last good day before ..."

"Before what?"

Before I'm blind, I thought, the words too horrifying to utter out loud.

"Before autumn," I said.

JD nodded and shrugged. I could not give voice to the possibility that by winter I would lose my sight. The "Last Good Day," as I would forever come to refer to it, could not be darkened by fatalistic premonitions and so I slapped his knee and suggested we go down the hill to the lake and drink the sixpack chilling in the cooler. Never one to argue over the interruption of an awkward sentimental moment, let alone an invitation to throw back a cold one, JD grinned. He stood and opened the driver's side door. Whistling at Nora and Susanna, he made a tipping motion towards his lips and pointed to his watch-less wrist. Nora smiled and hoisted herself and her camera bag into the passenger's seat. Agreeing that "beer o'clock" was approaching, Susanna crawled over the tailgate into the truck bed and waved for me to join her.

I wiped the corners of my eyes with the hem of my T-shirt, planted a foot on the rear hitch, and pulled myself up beside her. Our tree's long shadow fell across the gravel road and JD stopped short of it as he exited the inlet, slowing our departure, lingering in the way that always feels necessary when bidding an old friend farewell. We shielded our eyes with our hands against the western sun, its blinding corona encircling the top most branches and, with a premonition as cold and as certain as death itself, I knew I would never see my lone tree again.

My gaze fell to the tall ditch grass that bent lazily in the light breeze that flowed up the hill from the lake. A snake's round polished head materialized between the faded green blades. He flicked his tongue, testing the air for signs of what lay in his path before he emerged and slithered through the gravel. He disappeared for a moment back into the ditch, then reappeared, his rapid movements carving a line of S-shaped symbols in the dust. His body was as big around as my forearm and at least three times as long. Not counting the unfortunate inmates at the Reptile Gardens, I had never seen a snake of his immense size. Even the occasional glimpse of a small Gardner snake was a rarity in these parts, and I motioned for Susanna, excitedly pointing over the side of the truck at the incredible creature. She tilted her head towards the spot, but wrinkled her brow.

"What am I supposed to be looking at?" she said.

The snake darted into the weeds for a moment, the rear half of his glinting black body still visible against the pale pea gravel.

"There," I said, jabbing my finger at the scaly spear of tail twitching tiny puffs of dust in its wake."The King snake. You can't miss him. He's at the edge of the ditch!"

She tried again, but only shook her head.

"Sorry, but I don't see him. He must have gone back into the ditch."

I nodded, my eyes never leaving the parting Brome grass as the reptile's head plunged forward onto the road and his tail vanished among the wild roses. He could not be transformed into the dark ribbons of blood that had invaded my vision. He wasn't the shadow of the tree's bare branch creeping across the switch grass, a fallen clump of earth from a farmer's plow, a decaying corn stalk, a misplaced cat tail blown west by a summer storm; logic dictated all as possibilities, but he wasn't any of them, either. As the truck began to roll, the snake stopped and coiled in the wheel rut of the field inlet, his slender head rising above the ground cherry and mustard weed. The primordial chill of a million evolutionary years seeped from the slits of his eyes and his stare clung to my skin, making it prickle.

You came for me, I thought. Only for me.

The fork of his tongue danced in the hot dusty air and as the truck picked up speed and my tears blurred the wild roses, the tree, and the snake, I had wondered if it was my terror he was tasting.

***

Daniel pushed the bowl of chili away without tasting it, and complained of a sour stomach and high blood sugar. I poured the untouched soup back into the pot without comment as he left the table. The kidney disease had made nausea and vomiting a regular occurrence and, although the dialysis had helped, Dan's system still struggled to function normally. The headaches, shortness of breath, and skin eruptions would remain until Dan's transplanted kidney began to pick up the slack.

I sat at the kitchen table alone and finished the dinner I was no longer hungry for as I listened to the icy flakes of snow blow against the window, my worries piling up, one after another. It was after ten when we arrived home from the hospital and I still had a chapter to prepare for class the next morning. Daniel had not eaten dinner and would probably have a hypoglycemic episode in the middle of the night. We were running low on insulin and I needed to stop at the pharmacy. Daniel had an appointment at the transplant clinic tomorrow afternoon. The dishes needed washing, the floor needed vacuuming, the laundry needed folding. I dropped my head against the back of the chair and exhaled. Sometimes it was too overwhelming: all of mine, all of his, all of it. It was in these moments that I felt Daniel's monster conferring strength to its hideous twin, their combined potency swallowing me from the inside out. I kneaded the knots in my neck as the advice Alicia had once offered fell like a shadow.

***

"Rumor has it you and Daniel Levin are shacking up," she had said, as she leaned forward in her wheelchair and whispered conspiratorially into my ear.

"We're sharing an apartment," I said.

"Sharing like roomates?"

"No, not like roommates. Like … well, what you said. I guess we're shacking up."

She giggled girlishly. Alicia had once divulged that if she was younger and not happily married, she would have snatched Daniel for herself. His charm and boyish good looks had attracted attention from many of the females, both blind and sighted, at the rehabilitation center. Alicia and I were not the only women enamored with him. She stopped laughing, a serious thought suddenly seeming to damper her amusement, and grasped my arm. The gesture startled me.

"Please don't misunderstand when I say this, because I am glad for you. You've both been through so much and deserve happiness," she began, and then paused for a moment, moved her hand from my arm, and held my fingers instead."But I feel, as your friend, that I should share my concerns."

I tensed and prepared to receive the news that Daniel was messing around with one of the girls at the center or that he was leading a double life as a closeted gay man seeking social acceptability. Her tone seemed to insinuate that any number of heart-breaking scenarios were possible.

"Two diabetics in one house seems like one too many," she said."That's twice the low blood sugars, twice the high blood sugars, and twice as much moodiness—"

"I know all that," I snapped, interrupting her litany, as the years my mother had lived with my father and me played in fast reverse.

Annoyed by the icy bucket of reality she had thrown on the hormonal high of Daniel's and my cohabitation, I pulled my hand from hers. The ugly questions rose to the surface, not thwarted by my efforts to bury them. Why had my mother left my father? She had reassured me time and again that it had nothing to do with his diabetes. Did I believe her? Were my choices based on some bitter need to prove my own ability to remain loyal to a diabetic man?

Alicia began again, sweet and maternal."No relationship is easy. Look at Rich and me. We've had it tough over the years. Real tough."

Alicia, the great granddaughter of Swedish immigrants, had met Richard Teal in the college bookstore her senior year. His fingers, the luxurious color of mahogany, had brushed her pale wrist as they reached for the same volume of poetry.

"Do you find him as brilliant as I do?" he had said, offering her the ee cummings collection.

She'd smiled and taken the book from him. He thought better of it for a moment, then, directed by something far more powerful than apprehension, returned the grin, surprised to find warmth in such blue eyes. Five years after three civil rights workers were murdered in Mississippi and two years after their chance "next to, of course, god, America..." meeting, Richard Teal, without the blessing of his father, her parents, and most of their acquaintances, married Alicia Johansson in the dimly lit back room of a Minneapolis court house.

"We've drawn hate and resentment from every direction. But we've always known, no matter what we're confronted with during the day, at night, when we close the door behind us, racism remains outside. That disease, that monster, isn't allowed in," Alicia said, finding my hand again and squeezing it.

I tried to cut her short, seeing where she was headed, but she continued without pause. Her point sank deeper and deeper until the words at last struck the appropriate nerve.

"Two monsters. Daniel's diabetes and yours. You'll be living with them both because they won't ever let you leave *them* at the door."

***

I hesitated at the door of the bedroom and listened to Daniel's deep, even breathing. I moved silently around the foot of the bed, sliding piles of folded clothes into the dresser drawers and retrieving his rumpled shirt from the floor. He stirred in his sleep and I froze, suddenly terrified that he might wake up, might ask me when I was coming to bed. With the nervous twitch of a midnight intruder, I dropped the shirt back on the carpet, unwilling to risk the squeak of the closet hinges or the muffled crackle of fabric hitting the wicker hamper. As the lightness of my steps carried me forward, the heaviness of my guilt threatened to pull me back, until my hand caught the door frame and I stopped, searching for reasons why I shouldn't run, reasons that could evoke feelings of love born from a purer source than pity.

I returned to Daniel's side of the bed and sat next to him. He had fallen asleep on top of the comforter, his fist curled under his chin and a page of Braille lecture notes beneath his arm. Picking up the wrinkled sheet of paper, I smoothed the creases, placing it on the night stand. He wore only a thin pair of pajama pants and I unfolded a quilt to cover him.

As I wrapped it around his bare shoulders, my knuckles brushed against the cool rubber tubing snaking from his chest and my throat tightened, as if the line had risen from under the blanket and coiled around my neck like a constrictor. Fighting back the revulsion I hated myself for feeling, I ran my fingers over his thick brown hair and leaned

129

close, placing my lips to his forehead. I told myself all the necessary lies, providing a temporary emotional sedative. In that moment, as I lingered with my face pressed to Daniel's, I almost believe them: the snake could not hurt me, I could live with two monsters, and the kiss wasn't really a kiss good-bye.

CHAPTER SEVENTEEN

SPRING OF
THE STONE FEATHER

The broken piece of jasper lay in my hand and I squeezed it, the rough surface biting into my palm. Frederick Lightening Cloud gathered stacks of exams from the cluttered desktop. Retrieving a file folder from under his favorite stained coffee mug, he deposited the papers into it and tossed it down on the battered sofa cushion beside me. Fred had inherited the cast-off couch when he took the position as Dakota language and culture instructor and moved into the cubbyhole office in the basement of the American Indian Studies Department.

Although the old couch occupied almost a third of the room and the tiny window didn't offer much of a view, the space was a comfortable refuge and every time I entered I felt at peace among the powwow posters, the faint scent of sage and sweet grass, and the shelves lined with the literature of Luther Standing Bear, Ella Deloria, and Dee Brown.

"Can you finish correcting those and return them to the students by the end of the week?" Fred asked as he stretched to pick up the receiver of the ringing telephone. One of his long black braids fell off his substantial belly, dangling dangerously close to his coffee.

I nodded, rotated the stone, and discovered the points at each end. Frederick Lightening Cloud had done what other professors I had queried were not willing to do: he had hired me as his teaching assistant. I had approached him in the final days of the semester the previous year, but hadn't allowed myself too much hope, regardless of my superior grades in the beginning Dakota language class. Even a perfect academic performance in abnormal psychology had not been an adequate display of my capabilities for the last instructor I had queried. She had stammered, careful not to use the words "blind" or "disabled." She obviously knew the ground rules concerning discriminatory practices. Carefully, she asked if I considered myself qualified.

Having researched the required duties, I was prepared to explain in detail how I, as a blind person, would handle each responsibility, and I assured her of my competency. In the tone she might have use with a small child who is overly eager to help mother in the kitchen, she thanked me for my interest and said that she would call if she "thought of anything" I "could do". The call never came and I placated my wounded ego with the assumption that a more qualified student had been chosen. I would have labored on in the safety of this notion had it not been for the chance meeting with a well-meaning acquaintance early the next semester.

"Weren't you going to apply for the TA position in Dr. Lazarre's class?" He asked."I'm taking abnormal on Tuesdays and Thursdays. She doesn't have an assistant yet."

I bit the inside of my cheek until I tasted blood. Contempt flared into a firestorm that rushed through my thoughts, incinerating every benefit of the doubt I had ever imparted to Dr. Rachel Lazarre, Ph. D.

"I told Lazarre that I have a friend who was interested and she said that she really needs the help. You should apply. You'd be great."

Smiling weakly at his encouragement, I had thanked him for the tip, too numb to explain the bigoted back-story.

Although Frederick Lightning Cloud did not hold a doctorate in any specific field, he was intelligent enough to understand that even the assistance of a blind woman was far better than no help at all. His round face had beamed with genuine pleasure at the suggestion.

"I'm really excited that you want to work with me next semester," he said."I thought that you would be the best person for the job, but I didn't want to ask. Didn't want to make you feel pressured. I know just taking this class as a student has been challenging. But considering you didn't have the text in Braille, you've done well. You've learned the Dakota language in the traditional way. No books, no writing. Just listening and talking. I've been impressed with how quickly you've picked it up, like you were raised among fluent speakers."

"Pidamayaye," I said, blushing and then thanking him for the compliment.

"I had to listen to the message you left on my phone the other day twice. The first time I heard it, I thought you were this woman I knew when I was a boy on the reservation. Thought she was calling from Sisseton. Then I realized it was you and felt proud that I am your teacher. I think that grandmother in South Dakota would feel proud, too."

Fred never asked how I intended to grade papers or how I would proctor exams, sometimes trusting in my ability to adapt my skills to his tasks more than I did. But the gratitude I had for him became the dedication that never allowed me to fail. I found readers who, with my instruction, would spell each word of the language assignments, as I listened, making note of errors. It was an arduous process, but one that ended with great satisfaction when I handed the graded papers to Fred the next morning. Most of the students soon lost their apprehension at the idea of a blind assistant in the classroom and a few became regulars in the study lounge during my office hours. Fred and I shared their joy when my tutoring paid off and they passed their oral exams. As the year progressed, Frederick Lightening Cloud became more than a teacher, more than an employer; he became my mentor and my friend.

We unraveled our tales for one another, sometimes over black coffee and other times over draft beer. He recounted the horrors he had survived during his tour in Vietnam, remembering the terror of being a teenage combat soldier. I shared the stories of my blindness. He told me of his childhood in Sisseton, his mother's fight to keep him out of an Indian boarding school, and the sadness he felt when his family moved to Minneapolis where he and his siblings were plunged into the abject poverty, violence, and alcoholism that stain the urban Indian community.

For the first time, I spoke of my Grandpa Jack's admission of our heritage.

"So you are Indian," he said in a way that made me think he had known it all along.

"I don't know. Does that make me Indian?" I had asked, wanting it to be so, but afraid I had offended someone whose native identity was so undeniable.

"You've probably figured out by now, having worked and studied in this department, that the answer to that question depends on who you ask. For some, tribal enrollment and an ID card that says Red Lake or White Earth or Sisseton-Wahpeton on it are the only things required."

Sighing, he leaned his elbows on the table and continued. "But I've seen enough young punks with Cleveland Indian baseball caps and one of those cards in their pockets selling crack in our neighborhoods. I've watched women, carrying those same cards, dancing in a jingle dress in the pow wow circle on a Saturday afternoon. Then they go home, drink a couple bottles of cheap wine, and smack their kids around."

He paused and fixed his eyes on some place that didn't visibly exist in the room, a place haunted with ghosts of his past and his future. "I've never known people who lived in the traditional way to wave those papers in anyone's face. They may have had them, but they don't choose to attach their identity to it. Some will argue that enrollment status is important so we can hold on to the little land and resources we have, and it has gotten brutal since casino money muddied the waters. I have a different take on it."

I sipped coffee and encouraged him to elaborate.

"When those pieces of paper determine who is and who isn't an Indian, they also decide who benefits from casino money, natural resource profits, and tribal land holdings. In some cases, the smaller the number of people enrolled, the larger the payout per person. I suppose that works when it comes to gambling revenue, but what about the land? Wouldn't you say that's the most important, the most sacred?"

I nodded my agreement. To a native traditionalist, the land was more than an asset; it was "Mother".

"The problem lies with the tribal and federal government's definition of who qualifies as an Indian." He explained blood quantum and how, as enrolled tribal members married outside the tribe, the next generation did not receive recognition as Indians.

"As soon as the enrolled membership decreases, the government feels justified in seizing any land they consider surplus. With this kind of pedigree mentality, perhaps, someday, at least on paper, we will no longer exist."

As the words sank in, a sour sensation rose in my gut, the insidious implication affirming that the United States' genocide against Native Americans had not ended at Wounded Knee.

Fred's voice lifted to a more jovial tone as the waitress came by and filled our cups."Here's how ridiculous it all is. When I was born, my mother delivered in a hospital, which for the time and my family being Dakota, was uncommon. The doctor got confused when he filled out the birth certificate. In the section marked "race", there were only two choices: White or Negro. I obviously did not fit into either category, but feeling obliged to complete every detail, he decided that I should be "White". My mother told me this story when I was a boy, and my family had a good laugh about it, but it slipped my mind over the years. Then, when I enlisted in the army, the documentation declaring my whiteness resurfaced. It really screwed up the geniuses in the recruiting office."

I smiled and shook my head, my thoughts revolving to an earlier incident in our class. That day, the lesson had included a practice dialogue and, as was the usual drill, Frederick had gone around the circle of students, posing a question to each, a question which, as it grew closer to being my turn, had caused perspiration to rise on my neck. My heart pounded wildly. It was not that I didn't understand the words or their meaning. The language had, with its unusual guttural sounds and infixed verb conjugations, come surprisingly easy to me, as if it had been locked away in a secret part of my cellular memory, waiting for the right teacher to tap the knowledge. The apprehension arose from my uncertainty of which response best reflected the truth. Fred Lightning Cloud had reached the desk next to mine and asked my friend Rita the question.

Always confident, always cool, she lifted her beautiful face, her dark brown hair swinging loose from the beaded barrette her husband had crafted for her, and responded with a sense of pride that gripped my heart. Indecision swirled through my mental pathways like fog. The instructor praised her pronunciation, turned to me, and aimed the interrogative arrow.

"*Danikota he.*"

Are you Dakota? Are you Indian? The blood raced like fire in my veins, the answer beating in my chest and the spark that my grandfather had passed on all those years before blazed. *Han, Damakota ye.* Yes, I am Indian. The words pounded in my center, rising to my tongue, almost reaching my lips. But doubt began to creep in, muffling the clarity of my affirmation. I had not been raised on the Rosebud reservation like Lola, the woman across the class room. I had not grown up attending pow wows like Rita. Nick, the man sitting at the head of the circle, had a document stating his grandfather's identity. All I had ever possessed was Grandpa Jack's word. I had begun learning the culture, the spirituality, the traditions much later than my classmates, but I connected more strongly to what I had come to know than anything my white upbringing had ever provided.

Still, I was afraid to respond, afraid that if I gave name to what my heart knew as truth it would somehow diminish or disrespect those who had always lived within the sacred hoop. My blood screamed the answer, *I am Dakota. I am Indian.* But as misgivings about my Native American peers' presumptions magnified, my voice, although almost a whisper silenced my heart.

"Hiya, Damakota sni ye"

Frederick Lightning Cloud lingered for a moment as if he thought I might say something more, something different, but I didn't speak, dropping my sightless gaze to my lap, and he moved to the next student without comment. Although I was glad that I didn't have to see his face, blindness couldn't shield me from the profound disappointment conveyed in his silence. It had been all wrong: the answer, my reasons for giving it, the heart, like cold stone, that lay, stifled by betrayal, beneath my breast.

A vague recognition brushed the fringes of my memory as I traced the stone with my fingertip. Frederick replaced the receiver in the phone's cradle and opened the office window. It let in the scent of moist earth awakening beneath the melting snow.

"De taku he."

Asking for him to identify the object he had given me on my arrival to his office, I extended my open palm to Frederick Lightning Cloud. He took it and sat back down at his desk.

"Sdodyaya sni he," he said, seemingly surprised that I was unable to recognize the stone.

"No, I don't know," I said, then embarrassed by my ignorance, stated what I suspected was too obvious of an answer, *"Inyan."*

"Yes, it is a stone, but it's more than that. Don't you remember giving this to me?"

For a moment, I was a girl again, standing at the shore of Silver Lake. My braids dip into the frigid water. The receding ice reveals old treasures. Collecting the ancient pottery shards and broken pieces of flint from the sand, I place them gently inside a small leather pouch. I walk alone and listen to the lapping waves and the wind dancing along the fence where the black ridges of tilled field encroach on the sliver of hidden beach. The red-winged blackbirds trill in the cat tails. It is simple, this spring ritual, but it is sacred. It is my ceremony.

The sun climbs higher in the eastern sky and I stop to appreciate its warmth on my bare arms. The light sparkles on the water's surface and I catch sight of something out of the corner of my eye, something perfect, something wonderful. I roll my jeans to the knees and wade slowly towards it. I hold my breath, hoping it is not an illusion, hoping that the icy water is not deeper than I thought. For an instant, I lose sight of it among the hundreds of different colored stones.

Standing very still, my eyes strain and my feet grow numb, but soon the light illuminates the crystal clear water again and I see the object half buried in the sand. I wade deeper, the water rising past my knees, past my thighs. Finally reaching the spot, I plunge my arm up to the shoulder and grasp the sacred relic in my fist. I do not unclench my fingers until I am squatting on the beach, my braids dripping onto the soaked jeans. Time has worn the edges dull, but it is whole and unbroken.

I remember giving you the arrowhead," I said to Frederick, "but that doesn't look like it."

"It has been transformed. It once was stone. Then it was an arrow. Now it is something new," he explained, placing it back in my hand."It is an eagle feather."

I touched the pointed ends, the ridges, the grooves, and then recognized what I had been unable to see before. I gave it to him and asked if he had carved the design. He said that he had not.

"I always carried the arrowhead with me and yesterday when I arrived at the office, I pulled my keys out of my pocket and it fell and hit the floor. It broke into several pieces, but I could only find the one. I felt really sick about it until I brought the piece inside and looked at it in the light. When I saw what had happened, I realized my mistake wasn't really a mistake at all."

"You freed the feather," I said as I rose to leave.

He stood and rested his hand on my shoulder."I know who you are," he said, turning the stone object over in his palm, "Don't be afraid to follow your path."

The phone rang again, but Frederick Lightning Cloud did not answer it.

"*Oieihakewin*," he said.

I turned around. Last Word Woman. The sound of his voice saying it always added power to my name

"Danikota he"

Spring had arrived. The ice was receding and the water had never been clearer. Those things, ancient and buried were rising to the surface, revealing that which should never be forgotten. My heart and voice replied as one.

"Han, Damakota ye. Yes, I am Indian."

CHAPTER EIGHTEEN

AUTUMN OF
THE YELLOW ROSES

The monotone voice of the computer's screen reading software spat out a torrent of random letters and numbers which summoned my wandering mind's attention. Startled by the sudden noise and the sensation of a wet nose against my chin, I lifted Maakwa off of the keyboard and sat him on the floor at my feet. He purred and rubbed his furry black face against my ankle until I reached down to scratch between his ears.

"It looks like you wrote more today than I did, buddy," I said as I shut down the computer."Let's go find some dinner."

Scampering to the kitchen, Maakwa waited beside his empty dish and I rose from the aluminum folding chair and massaged the sensation back into my rear end while I silently cursed the ass-torturing metal seat. The hour spent at my desk had not amounted to much and, as easy as it would have been to blame the make shift desk chair, discomfort wasn't the source of my lull in creativity. The short story I had been working on still wasn't finished and as hard as I had tried to focus my attention on the characters, the conflict, and the climax, I found myself lost, lured away from both the world I was constructing with words and the world in which I lived.

My preoccupation had begun when I awoke from a dream that morning and it had persisted all afternoon. The man's image kept replaying: I had seen the angles of his face as the hot water jetted from the shower head, and my neck tingled under the deluge; as I balanced a basket on my hip, I had flashed on the brownness of his smooth skin while the elevator descended ten floors to the laundry room; his many slender black braids had stroked my memory as I absently washed an already clean glass; and my fingers had not moved from home row to create a single sentence, his handsome, but rarely-seen smile turning my own lips into the grin that, to my relief, only Maakwa had witnessed. He had arrived in the dream during the seconds just before dawn, but, unlike so many other faces that visited my sleep, his did not fade with the sunrise. It became more vivid, more real until I wondered if the dream man might manifest, leaping through the thin veil that separated one reality from another, in the room. Would his face hover above mine as it had the night before? Would I feel his hands beside my cheek and the tips of his braids sweeping my neck? Could the passion this man conjured exist beyond the dream's boundary? Afraid of the profound disappointment that always followed unrealistic expectations, I refused to entertain the fantasy.

Sleep was the sweet sanctuary where I still saw the cool blue of the sky, the crisp green grass, and the bleeding heart flower's candy-pink petals. There, I could again see the sparkle in my mother's eyes when she laughed. The contours of my father's chin, the curve of his jaw, and the lines of the face that resembled my own were clear and bright. In dream time, my grandfather waved through a window as he fed fat red squirrels handfuls of cracked yellow corn. He wore a black sweat shirt, the one with the Harley Davidson emblem. Jumping into my beat up Chevy Vega, I dreamed that I threw the white cane into the backseat and drove down Highway 9, the radio blaring a Neil Young song. "Old Man, look at my life," I sing along, "I'm a lot like you."

But then morning came, I opened my eyes, and it all disappeared. My waking reality could not afford belief in improbable fantasies, and sensuality, like sight, had become a gift given only by sleep, received only in slumber. The man with the intense eyes and furtive smile lived in that place, the place where dreams were born, and it was impossible for him to break through the cordon that separated him from my waking world.

The crash of breaking glass and angry shouts filtered through the thin apartment wall. The man next door was drinking again and I knew that soon, as was the usual custom, he would move the chaotic scene into the hallway. I paused at the open refrigerator and listened anxiously to the escalation of the fight. I slid a knife from the kitchen drawer, moved to the front door and touched each lock to make sure the bolts were secure. The argument grew more heated and a piece of furniture, or perhaps one of the drunk men, collided into the wall with a sickening thud. A slurred string of profanity and threats of violence followed. Laying down the knife, I went to the dining table and picked up the phone. I dialed 911 and ran my fingers through Maakwa's thick coat as I waited for an operator to answer. Another series of crashes echoed through the wall. The cat rose to his haunches and stared at it with wide green eyes as if he could see the spectacle through the paint and sheet rock. I reported the situation and hung up, with hope that the police would be there soon. They were more than a little familiar with the address.

The building's units had been reserved for seniors and the disabled, until the low income housing waiting lists were choke with thousands of names. With demand far greater than supply, the Housing Authority redefined the qualifications for eligibility, first including more tenants with mental illness or substance abuse problems. But the waiting list kept growing until, with no better solutions from which to choose, they finally offered living space to the general population of low income applicants. They moved in, lugging their cardboard boxes of meager belongings along with a bitter sense of desperation, petty theft and domestic violence its byproducts. The Marie Avenue high-rise soon became a frequently visited location of the South St. Paul police.

The neighbor's apartment door slammed and the drunks tumbled out into the hallway just as the elevator stopped in the vestibule. Two officers stepped around the corner and seized the men, who, from the sounds of it, were rolling on the floor in a vicious embrace. Hauling them to their feet, the cops escorted my foul-mouthed neighbor and his unfortunate drinking buddy downstairs and, as the elevator door slid closed, I released the breath I held. No one had been shot or had "accidentally" fallen to their death down the elevator shaft. The violence had been kept to a minimum this time.

I sat at the table, tense and unable to eat the leftovers getting cold on the plate in front of me, and began to wonder if my mother was right. Perhaps the ten years I had survived the city was proof enough of my independence. Maybe it was time to go home.

"You wouldn't have to live with us," she had said after I admitted that I needed a change."You could apply for one of those nice low income apartments in Lake Park. You'd only be a few blocks from Grandma and Grandpa. The grocery store is in walking distance, too."

Taking my silence as agreement with her suggestions, she had tentatively moved on to much shakier ground."Maybe you would even consider going to church. They have activities for singles and it might be a good way to meet someone special."

She hadn't been able to hide her eagerness and I had been incensed by the suggestion. I viewed a return to the rural town where I had grown up as a failed finish to my battle for dignity and self-determination. But as my college career ended and my thirtieth birthday came and went, I began to lose sight of my purpose, my reason for it all, and the idea seemed less like the retreat of a coward and more like an unfulfilling, but sensible, option on which to settle. I had accumulated too many nights of television reruns and audio books, resigned to the idea that the cat, curled at the foot of my bed, was the only male companionship I needed or deserved. Reminders of the contentment I lacked came in the mailbox, disguised as friends' wedding, baby shower and house warming invitations. I attended, expressing an appropriate amount of spectator joy over their first kiss as a married couple, their infant's tiny grasping fingers, or their suburban split level.

The forced smiles quickly became aching facial cramps and I hurriedly retreated to my cracker box apartment. There, I could fall into my empty bed, contemplate my empty bank account, and weep, a hand pressed to my empty womb. During the darkest hours, I poised at the edge of the precipice, the tips of my toes touching the interface of solidity and air, and I would, when I dared to glance into the abyss, catch sight of my mother's safety net outstretched below. But regardless of how close loneliness pushed me towards the rim, I didn't take the leap. I dreaded that I would not only be caught by the net, I would also be captured in it.

Balanced on the apartment's window ledge, Maakwa sniffed the brisk October wind whining through the window cracks. The last few leaves clung to the elm branches in the courtyard below and their brittle rustling echoed like the slow steady shake of a ceremonial rattle. I joined him at the glass and felt Maakwa's tail twitching as he crouched low and laid his ears flat. A formation of geese flew across the dusky sky line, so near the high-rise's window I heard the flapping wings. Maakwa shot up on his hind legs to paw at the glass, but the birds stayed on their course, honking as if amused by the cat's comical attempt at a pursuit.

"Do you want to fly south for the winter, too?" I said, as Maakwa lost his footing and slipped off the ledge into my arms.

He freed himself, jumped back onto the sill, and cried after the departing geese, I patted him, understanding his disappointment.

"Don't be sad," I said, more soothed by the sentiment than my feline companion, whose head remained pressed against the window."You can follow them in dreamtime."

In the nights that followed, the man with the many braids and the inviting smile returned to my dreams. Standing at the bottom of a steep hill, I watched as he descended from the crest at an incredible speed, gliding down like wheels were attached to his feet. He cradled an arm full of yellow roses and, as he flew more rapidly towards me, our collision seemingly unavoidable, he tossed the flowers into the air. Catching me around the waist, he came to a halt and pulled me closer. Yellow petals fell around us like rain and I saw myself reflected in the deep pools of his dark pupils. In his eyes, I saw beauty, I saw peace, I saw love. My lips drew towards him, my head light with anticipation of his kiss, the air heavy with the intoxicating perfume of roses. But before our mouths could meet, a gentle, yet persistent, caress against my cheek tugged me from our embrace and, reeled from the dream by the paw of a playful cat, I reluctantly returned to the waking world.

I rolled out of bed, shaky and disoriented from the premature reentry and Maakwa parked on the shaft of sunlight streaming through the window onto the rumpled pillow. Not quite sure which world I was walking around in, I stumbled to the kitchen, hoping to find the man and his yellow roses. All that greeted me was an empty coffee pot and a box of stale cereal. But, as I scooped grounds into a filter and filled the pot with water, I could still feel his arms pressing against the small of my back, petals clinging in my hair, and the all-consuming desire to know his kiss.

The strong coffee helped sort my shuffled thoughts and rationalize the reason behind the dream man's reoccurring appearance. I supposed that it was not unusual for a single lonely woman to create through dreams the lovers she was missing in her life. The dreamscape was always the perfect clandestine point to rendezvous with those individuals we found attractive in the waking hours, but could not, for one reason or another, approach. It also was the fertile ground for those flawless nameless beings who were created for and existed exclusively in the dreamer's sleep.

The problem, however, was that the man with the many braids did not fit into either category, a fact which disturbed, mystified, and awakened a thousand butterflies from forgotten cocoons. We had never met, never seen the other's face, never spoken. But he was not an imaginary figment created in my sleep. He existed in the waking world, as real as the cup of coffee in my hand, as real as the cat sleeping on my bed. Beyond the intimacy of the dream, we were unfamiliar to one another, and yet I knew his name. I had known his name for years.

***

Rita listed off names as she stood one hand on her hip, at the grocery meat counter.

"There's Carl, the kids, you, Carl's brother," she said, pausing briefly and turning to me."How many bratwursts would you buy for the game on Sunday?"

"I would cook at least a dozen," I said, as I tackled Roland, who tried to wiggle free of the cart's child safety seat."No, little man, Auntie says you have to sit while your Mommy shops!"

Folding up my cane, I handed it to him and grabbed the wrapped bundle of paper plates from the basket.

"Sing something for Auntie," I said and kissed his round face.

Carl had covered the top of my cane with several rows of peyote stitch bead work and when Roland wasn't teething his gums on it he preferred to use it as a drumstick. He yanked it from his mouth, beat a strong rhythm on the shrink-wrapped plates, and, sporting the most adorable toothless grin, started to sing.

"Carl must have taught him that one, huh, Rita? That does not sound like Dakota to me."

Laughing, she tossed the packages of brats in the basket. "Yeah, I think Carl corrupted him with some crazy Ojibwa words," she said, and tickled Roland's plump baby fat. "Dakota dowan!"

Roland ignored his mother's request to sing in her native language and continued in what could only be translated as "toddler".

"Who are you going to cheer for on Sunday, Vikings or Bucs?"

Rita had grown up in Florida and had moved to Minnesota when she met Carl. She was more than my friend. She had become my sister. Together, we had learned our people's language, studying long hours in practice conversations and with spontaneous vocabulary quizzes. Walking across campus and hearing a barking dog, I would ask in Dakota for her to identify the source of the sound. Usually fueled with a surplus of devilish wit, she would respond with flawless diction that it was my boyfriend or my father or my dinner. She never passed on a joke, a prank, or a juicy tidbit of gossip, calling the latter "dirt".

"What's the dirt?" she would say at the beginning of every phone call, shopping trip, or lunch date.

Riding with Rita during her first Minnesota winter had given me a new appreciation for seat belts; Rita's unselfish sharing of the ups and downs of pregnancy and parenthood had given me a new appreciation of children. She had lent comfort through my rocky relationships. I had lent comfort through her marital spats. She possessed a voluptuous figure, abundant self confidence, beautiful children, and an adoring doting husband. Rita embodied everything I was not and I admired her greatly.

"Simple," she said, as she loaded bags of chips on top of the football party grocery heap. "When I'm in Minnesota, I cheer the Vikings. When I visit Tampa, I'm a Bucs fan."

"Come on, Rita, it's me you're talking to. Screw the family diplomacy. Who do really want to win?"

She lowered her voice to a whisper as if she thought Carl may have wire tapped her purse. "The Bucs. How about you?"

"Neither one. I'm a Bears fan," I said.

"So you're just coming to my house for the food?"

"That's right, Sister. Your brother-in-law's bringing his barbeque ribs?"

"Sure, he always does. But I hear he's leaving his girlfriend at home," she said, and elbowed my arm.

Rita was on a constant search for the perfect Indian man with whom to set me up, but, although she meant well, her skill as a matchmaker was less than amateur and often amusing. It had become a running joke rather than a serious search, as she whispered in my ear that a nice Ojibwa fellow was winking at me on our way into the Indian Center, advising that he had "most" of his teeth, or sharing that she'd met my future sweetheart at an intertribal basketball game and that all four of his ex wives thought he was a great guy.

"Which girlfriend will he be leaving at home this time?" I said."The one that slashed his tires or the one that gave him a black eye?"

"Cruel!" she mocked."I know you're in denial. Admit it and I'll tell him you want more than just his ribs."

The man at the cash register was shaking his head at our antics, Rita told me, as she puckered up and made vulgar kissing noises and I swatted her with my purse.

"Just ignore her bad behavior," Rita said, handing him the cash."She's in love."

"Your mother's lost her mind," I said, hoisting Roland from the cart as she wheeled the groceries to the van.

She slid him into his car seat, gave him a bottle of juice, and retrieved a box from the back. Laying it on my lap, she started the engine and exited the parking lot. I stuck my hand inside, "looking" at the contents: a plastic storage container I had brought salad in to Carl's birthday, a jacket I had forgotten at a powwow the weekend before, some refrigerator artwork drawn by their daughter, Julia, and a compact disc case.

"What's this?" I asked.

I pulled the case from under the crayon colored sheets of paper and held it in the sunlight shining through the windshield.

Rita glanced at it, made a left turn, and stopped in front of Julia's pre-school. Before she had a chance to respond, a group of little girls, full of giggles and shrieks, darted up the leaf-strewn sidewalk towards the van. Rita climbed out, slid the side door open, and Julia jumped in, twisting around the back of my seat to kiss my cheek.

"Auntie Amy," she said excitedly, "open your door! Hurry!"

"There are some curious four year olds out here who want to meet you," Rita said.

I dropped the compact disc back into the box and got out, unfolding my cane to the fascinated gasps of three little onlookers. Julia, utilizing the van's open side entrance as a stage, put her hand on my shoulder and addressed her classmates like a side show barker.

"This is my auntie," she said and I smiled at the possessive nature of her introduction."She's blind. She can't see, but she can do all kinds of stuff."

"What kind of stuff?" a sweet but skeptical voice challenged.

Julia hopped off the running board, her braids and beaded ear rings flying out behind her as she landed. She grasped my finger as if she thought I might try to escape her impromptu show and tell.

"She makes cookies for me. She doesn't make them for Roland because he's a baby. She just makes them for me and sometimes I let Mommy have one."

I felt a tug at my sweater sleeve and heard a shy request."Julia's Auntie, can I hold your stick?"

As if on cue, Julia broke in with a tone so similar to one often used by Rita, I chuckled."It's not a stick! It's a cane," my pint-size politically correct niece admonished.

"Yes, it's a cane and you may hold it," I said, and offered it to the small hand still clinging to my sleeve.

The gesture completely broke the ice and unleashed an avalanche of questions and comments.

"Do you have one of those dogs that show you where to go?"

"Do you know Stevie's grandma? She's blind, too."

"Can you see the sun?"

"Are you sad?"

"I think you're pretty."

"Do you know what color your sweater is?"

"Will you make us cookies?"

Roland, disgruntled with the fact that Julia's friends were not paying as much attention to him as usual, hurled his empty bottle out the van's side door. Rita retrieved it and told the girls it was time to take cranky little brothers home for a nap. As we drove away, she laughed at the scene outside the passenger window.

"They're waving at you, Julia's Auntie," she said.

I raised my hand and waved back. Three little mouths opened and six little eyes widened as if something mysterious, something magical had just occurred.

As the van crawled through St. Paul's early rush hour traffic, I passed the colored pictures to Julia and asked her to tell me about them. The first paper depicted a very large pink bird accompanied by a space ship. Both passed over a green building which she said was my house. Somehow, the odd pink bird brought the south-bound geese to mind while also invoking images of flamingos. Julia gave the picture back and considered the last one.

"It's you, Auntie. You're wearing a purple dress."

"And really big orange earrings," Rita chimed in."No daughter of mine would forget to accessorize."

Julia continued, "You're holding your cane and some flowers."

"What kind of flowers are they, Jules?" Rita inquired.

"The kind like daddy brought you, only not red."

"Those flowers are called roses, honey," Rita said.

"What color are my roses?" I said.

The van slowed to a stop in front of the high-rise and I took the drawing from her, and slid it into the box.

"Yellow," Julia said.

I blushed. A thousand buttery petals poured through dreamtime's veil, bringing the man's smiling face with them. A feeling began to build inside of me. It was the feeling I had once as a girl, when I rode an old wooden roller coaster with my father.

***

We went to Arnold's Amusement Park on the shores of Lake Okoboji every summer. It was a short drive from Lake Park and, although the seventies had tainted the landmark with seedy lake front biker bars and head shops disguised as souvenir stores, I loved the wooden floored roller rink, the salt water taffy shop, the mechanical metal arms pulling sticky pink ropes of candy in the store's front window, and the funhouse with the giant slide, crazy mirrors, and creepy organ playing clown. The August I was ten, I persuaded my father to take our annual visit while my mother attended a garden show. It was a rare occasion that we went places without her, but, to my surprise, he agreed to take me. Strolling passed the little novelty shops near the park's entrance, we silently browsed the souvenirs and curios, until I spotted a small carved cedar box, pointed at it and glanced hopefully up at my father's face. I didn't really expect him to buy it for me, which added to my astonishment when he picked up the little box and paid the shopkeeper for it. As we entered the amusement park and purchased tickets, although I thought myself too old, I held his hand.

Having never ridden a roller coaster, my stomach tightened before we even left the platform and I gripped the lap bar with both hands. My father said that he had not been on it since he was a boy, but, as he recalled, it was a thrilling ride for a first-timer. With his gift sitting on the seat between us, my leg pressed against it, our car began to climb upward. The grinding of chains and the old wooden structure's creaking fed my nervous anticipation as the incline steepened and we lifted above the tops of the oaks one jerky thrust at a time. Approaching the pinnacle, my father pointed to a faded sign suspended over the track. I squinted through the late afternoon sunshine at the peeling painted letters and the hairs stood up on my arms. Our car balanced at the top and I read the words above my father's head in the seconds before we tipped over the summit. Shrieks of laughter escaped from behind my broad smile, my father's hand covered my white knuckles, and we plummeted towards the Earth. Behind us, the "Point of No Return" swung back and forth on its rusted chains.

***

Rust red leaves skipped across the driveway as I stood at the open van door and withdrew the compact disc from the box. Rita said that it was a book she thought I would enjoy.

"Who's the author?" I asked, as the wind lifted my long hair off of my back and playfully tossed it over my shoulder.

"The kids' uncle, the one in Florida, wrote it. I've told you about him."

I nodded, the veil now so thin my mind's eye could see everything through it: a shiny steel car ascending a steep track, the man with many braids riding beside me, the book on the seat between us. As I balanced upon the emotional zenith, I anticipated the sound of his name and the brilliant breath-stealing free fall towards the place where all realities would become one.

Suddenly lost in the incredible sensation that I was not only falling, but also flying, I heard my own voice above the November wind. "Gabriel," I said.

And the veil vanished.

CHAPTER NINETEEN

SPRING OF
THE SACRED BUNDLE

The night jasmine filled the darkness with a scent so thick I could almost taste its sweetness. Beyond the jalousie window, the cicadas sang from the oaks and sable palms, drowning out the hum of the ceiling fan over the bed as the wooden blades slowly churned the room's sultry air. Gabriel cradled my head in the crook of his elbow and combed his fingers through my tousled hair, his lips brushing feathery kisses across my cheeks, nose, and chin. I reached through the dark to touch his face. He was smiling.

"Are you real?"

"Yes, I'm real and I love you," he said.

Outside, the insects' shrill whine faded and the tree frogs began to sing. A faint chirp rose from the vine covered fence beyond the window and, from behind the rows of books lining the corner shelf, a gecko replied to the call.

"When did you know that you loved me?" he asked.

I pulled free from the tangled bed sheet, rolled onto my hip, and kissed him. The sea salt still clung to our mouths as it had that afternoon when I dove beneath the blue- green surface and emerged into his waiting arms. It seemed as if one moment in time could not encapsulate my knowing. The union of our emotions had become the one great certainty of life, my one truth, and its confirmation sprang from every touch, every thought, every experience we shared, my adoration exceeding any limits I had ever imagined. How could I name the moment in which I fell? I was continuously falling.

I drew him to me and pressed his cheek to my breast, as my heart beat fast and my skin savored his warm breath. A pleasurable rush of recent memories washed through me and each moment, in its intense beauty, begged to be the answer to his question.

On the first evening of my arrival in the paradise the Spaniards had so aptly named the land of flowers, he had clasped my hand and led the way over the white dunes. The dragonflies hovered around us, sea grass and sea oats, paired with the wind as their partner, performed a slow graceful dance, and the Gulf of Mexico shimmered like a flawless turquoise jewel before us. Sliding off my sandals, my feet touched the sugary sand for the first time and we quickened our stride, the hypnotic sound of the breaking waves enticing us to the water's edge. As the sea curled forward and touched my toes, feet, and then ankles, in a wonderful new, yet soothingly familiar way, I was overcome with a similar joy as when I had first embraced Gabriel. Although the physical meeting had been introductory, it was a reunion with something, with someone I had always known in the most secret part of my soul.

We stood for a long time, my back to his chest, his arms encircling my waist, as the warm water lapped against our bare legs, until I no longer sensed a distinct separation between Gabriel, the sea, and myself. Like tiny simplistic offerings, tears streamed down my face, merging with the ocean, each small droplet fusing with the very source of my gratitude. As I turned towards Gabriel, wanting to express my appreciation to him for having given me such an incredible gift, I caressed his face and the sensation on my finger tips silenced my intended words. He had lived the better part of his life listening to the music of jingling sail clips swinging from their naked masts. The ebbing tide's pungency invoked his most comforting memory of infancy. For decades he had come to the shore to swim, to meditate, to write his books. But although he had returned to this stretch of beach a thousand times, for a thousand different reasons, as the setting sun cast its golden trail across the water where we stood, his tears had fallen, too.

"Was it when we went to the Gulf for the first time? Is that when you knew you loved me?" he said, as if he shared the thought in which I was immersed.

"I loved you then, it's true. More than I've ever loved anyone. But I knew before the beach. Before I came to Florida."

"It was the roses, wasn't it?"

I smiled in the darkness, remembering his time-honored method of traditional courtship and the dozen yellow roses that had arrived at my apartment door. The card said that he was sending the color of the Florida sunshine and all of his love. Not yet having told him of the dream of falling petals, I had mused over the mystical connection that seemed to coalesce our minds and hearts.

Only the Dakota word meaning sacred, mysterious, and holy could explain it. Our bond to one another was *wakan*.

"Yes, I fell in love with you that day, too," I said, "but the first moment, the moment when I knew you were the one came long before the roses or the Gulf or even before we touched."

He ran his hand along the curve of my shoulder, stroked the length of my arm, and brought his palm to rest on my waist. "When? What was it?"

"Your words. I fell in love with your words and the sound of your voice. When I heard them for the first time, something incredible happened. Something I had thought was impossible."

The waxing moon spread a translucent blanket of soft light over our bodies and I sensed his gaze searching for, and then finding my face in the shadows.

"Your words gave me sight," I said. "I could see the world again."

What is the world, if not magic? What is magic, if not the world?

***

Gabriel's voice had journeyed a thousand miles, the pages of his book transformed into sound. More like song than story, his prose whispered in my ears, the quiet and calming tone of his speech only magnifying the power of his words.

"Magic," I said, paused the volume for a moment, and lay back on the floor beside the compact disc player.

It defined Gabriel's appearance in my dreams. It defined the yellow roses in Julia's crayon portrait, it defined the inexplicable connection he and I, as virtual strangers, had to one another in such a vast universe of endless possibilities. Intuition flared and I pressed the play button, anticipating the release of a greater magic. His words flowed out of the speakers and into the room, not as the precise and measured reading of a written manuscript, but with the emotional attachment of a storyteller born from the oral tradition of our native ancestors. As he recounted ancient teachings, spoke of the sanctity of ceremony, and offered to the present and future generations the primal wisdom the generations that came before had gathered, any doubts I had ever harbored about my identity, my beliefs, my path dissolved, leaving only clarity. He named the feeling I had been carrying since childhood, the connective feeling of universal consciousness, the connection of myself to everything. The Great Holy Mystery. Wakan Tanka. And although I had heard the words before, they had never been so real, so tangible.

Wakan Tanka is in everything and everything is in Wakan Tanka.

His words brought the answers for which I had hungered my entire life and, insatiable, I listened to the lines over and over until the ceiling disappeared and his voice sculpted the night sky. A billion pinpoints of starlight twinkled across the black velvet, glimmering in my mind's eye. The quarter moon rose like a sharp silvery sickle. Sable palms and yellow pines replaced concrete walls and glass windows and the scuffed linoleum vanished beneath dunes of bone-white sand. Tropical sea breezes banished the Minnesota chill from the air as Gabriel's voice led me down trails covered with moss and carpets of pine needles to the site where the sea turtles lay their eggs.

The conviction behind his creation did not need the eye as intercessor to the world of which he wrote. It spoke directly to the spirit. Opening wide the eye of my mind to the beauty I had missed for so long and to the unrealized wonders my brief years of sight had never known, I experienced the sable palms and sea turtles as clearly as my visual memory of the moon and the stars.

When the book had ended, the beauty and the magic remained. His voice lingered in my thoughts, paired with the images from my dreams, and brought him further into my reality. It spawned such an intense feeling for the man and his creation that I was frightened and searched for something other to call it than what I knew it to truly be. When Rita asked if I had enjoyed her brother-in-law's writing, I called it "admiration". When she encouraged me to send a letter expressing this "admiration," I agonized over every line, every word, every syllable, calling it "veneration," "reverence," and "respect". But when his unexpected response came less than a day later, the many pages revealing his thoughts of my long hair as he watched the wind whipping the palm fronds and how he imagined the tropical sun warming my skin, I realized that we were on the unnervingly mysterious, yet blissfully exhilarating, head-long rush together and had finally called the feeling "love".

**

"I fell in love with your words, too," Gabriel said, his many long braids brushing my shoulders as they had done in the dream."Our words completed the connection that had already started in the Mystery. It began when I made my prayer bundle."

He slipped his legs from beneath our star quilt, rose from the bed, and crossed through the room's shadows to the shelves in the corner. A slow sensuous heat flowed like liquid fire beneath my skin, my imagination following his naked brown body through pools of moonlight. He was the man in the dream, magnified: more beautiful, more erotic, more stirring. Carefully moving aside conch shells, a braid of sweet grass, a small stone fetish of a dolphin, and a clay pot filled with hawk, crow, and owl feathers, he produced a leather pouch and returned with it. He sat on the side of the bed, holding the bundle gently in his large palm as if he were grasping a piece of sweet ripened fruit or a bird's egg. He spoke, his voice hushed and filled with sincerity.

"The love that I have always wanted, the kind I needed, has eluded me for most of my life. I tried to find it. Even thought I did a couple of times, but there was always something missing, leaving me unfulfilled. I spent thirty years resigned to the idea that I didn't deserve any better. That I deserved to be drained without ever being replenished. At some point, I decided that love wasn't worth the hurt that always seemed to come attached to it."

I reached out and stroked his back, with a wish that I possessed the power to protect him from his past. But I could not rescue him from the feeling of betrayal as one marriage ended in divorce nor could I erase the grief when another ended in death. I could no more free him from the bitter marital memories of adultery, alcoholism, uncontrolled anger, and abuse than he could save me from the monstrous disease that had stalked my childhood and robbed me of eye sight. Bound by the present moment, we could only cherish one another, feeling more thankful for content-ment and pleasure having once known chaos and pain.

"I didn't know whether I should continue on my path alone or if I should search for a companion. I struggled with it for a long time, not convinced that I would be happy living a solitary life, but I was too discouraged by my memories of what love had been like in the past. I felt too old, too tired, and the risk seemed too great."

He paused, and then stared at the space on the wall where a framed photograph of two handsome Indian men hung, bathed in the moon's glow."My indecision ended when I remembered what my uncles, Nip-pawanock and Metacomet taught me. They raised me to honor the ways of our ancestors."

Gabriel grew silent for a moment. The lessons of his boyhood stretched across forty years, and the memories of his beloved elders, their spirits now one with the Great Mystery, shifted him back to the time and place of his learning.

***

"I'm curious, Nephew," Nippawanock had said, as he peered over the books and papers piled on his desk at the boy standing in front of it."Which half of you is Indian?"

"What do you mean, Uncle?"

"Which half is it? Is it your front half or your back half? Your top half or your bottom half?"

Gabriel blushed and cast his gaze towards the floor. He suddenly rea-lized what his uncle must be referring to and couldn't bring himself to meet the man's intense blue stare. The English professor's eyes had on occasion caused a number of his University of South Florida students to squirm with discomfort as they pierced through flimsy excuses for late term papers and unsatisfactory exam scores.

Earlier that afternoon, when a boy cornered Gabriel outside his uncle's house, taunting and prodding, the response had seemed safe enough, acceptable enough. He had always hated the way some people felt that they had the right to interrogate him about his identity, his race, his tribe. Usually he chose to ignore the intrusive questions and would have done the same that day. But the situation had changed when he noticed a group of girls, including a pretty Cherokee schoolmate, who had stopped along the sidewalk to listen. Gabriel's female classmates had obviously not been the only ones listening.

"Our people do not come in parts," Uncle Nip said, leaning closer to his young nephew."Either you are Indian or you're not."

The boy looked into the man's eyes and found only warmth and sincerity. His uncle had understood the danger and degradation of having one's whole identity relegated to a number, signified by a fraction.

"The heart knows the answer. What is yours saying to you, Gabriel?"

Standing before his uncle, eyes closed, he acknowledged the undeniable, embracing his inner truth. It was a truth that had sustained him throughout his life, placing him on the path of heart and leading him to create the sacred object he now cradled in his hands.

***

"In the old way, I made my bundle," he said, as he caressed the smooth leather with the fingers of one hand and my hip with the other.

"Along with the tobacco, the sweet grass, and the special objects, I spoke my prayers, prayers for the one I had always wanted, the one that I needed to feel whole. Then I released it to the Mystery."

Smoothing his palm across my stomach, he untied the strip of leather that fastened the bundle and slowly shook its contents onto my bare belly. I carefully took a breath, feeling the dry flecks of tobacco and crumbling sage that clung to my skin and collected in the hollow of my navel. I resisted the welling urge to sift it through my fingers, wanting instead, to name each cool, each soft, each ridged, each rough, each smooth, each round piece with the part of my flesh onto which they had fallen.

"Only I knew what was in the bundle. I put it in a safe place and waited, knowing that I would either complete my path alone or," He hesitated and laid the empty pouch aside, "somewhere in the Mystery, the woman attached to this bundle would come and we would walk the path together."

He took one of the objects from the small mound, placed it in my hand and I closed my fingers around its curved edges.

"You are that woman."

He gathered me in his arms and the ceremonial reverence that had created the bundle, the magic that had delivered us into each other's dreams, and the power that exists in tenderness culminated, becoming heat, becoming energy, becoming passion. Sage leaves and sweet grass shifted between our bodies and the heady perfume of their crushed leaves infused the air. Night pulsed, everything hidden within its dark secret folds, breathing and sighing and singing. I squeezed the small fetish tighter as I released myself to all that is *wakan,* until

The heart, carved from stone, lay, warm and shiny, in my palm.

CHATPER TWENTY
AUTUMN OF JOSEPHINE

Gabriel down shifted the Mustang as we crossed the bridge from the mainland onto US-1. Blinking at the rays that broke through the coconut palms and crisscrossed the highway, he took his hand off of the gearshift and touched my knee.

"Welcome to the Keys," he said, as he drummed the steering wheel with his other hand and sang bits and pieces of the Beach Boys song that played on the radio.

I closed my hand over his and held it tightly.

"Beats November in Minneapolis doesn't it?" he said.

Sliding his fingers from under mine, he slipped on a pair of round wire rim sun glasses, adjusted the knot on the black bandana around his head, and stepped on the gas, the GT growling like a wary eight cylinder animal. Key Largo's pastel condos, parrot heads sipping rum and fruit juice outside beach bars, and shops crammed with tourists buying Panama hats to cover their already shockingly pink scalps blurred past the tinted windows. The aroma of boiled shrimp and fried grouper mingled with the scent of something floral and exotic and bombarded my senses with the heady fragrance of the tropics.

It had been several years since Gabriel had traveled the route with his youngest son, Carises, on their way to Grassy Key, and he scanned the island's crowded landscape, noting the many changes that had occurred since his last visit. In Florida, as it is wherever civilization has taken an aggressive foothold, creation and destruction are born of the same irresponsible parent. Housing developments rose, groves of thousand year old Cyprus fell. The mangroves and dunes vanished, replaced by sea walls constructed of concrete, a false sense of security, and man's arrogant belief that he can thwart the force of the sea, while, in the shadows, pragmatic politicians, real estate brokers, and energy company tycoons hid and divvied up the land they have never known and will never know as "Mother".

Suddenly, Gabriel quit tapping the steering wheel, an uncomfortable silence replaced the rhythmic beat, and a long moment passed before he spoke.

"They paved paradise ...."

The truth behind Joni Mitchell's lyrics made them a whole lot less catchy than "Wouldn't It Be Nice" and, after saying them, he grew quiet again. My thoughts journeyed two thousand miles north to the once empty expanse of beach along the south shore of Silver Lake, where, as a girl, I had retrieved the arrowhead from the cold spring water. But civilization had come for it, too, hemming it with curbs, gutters, street lights, and expensive new homes. The invisible fibers connecting my heart to ancestors, family, and the land of my birth yanked taught and I ached to feel the raking wind blowing across the flat broad corn fields and the slick stones of the lake shore beneath my bare soles.

"I'm sorry. I didn't mean to bring you down," he said, reading my distant expression."There's still pockets of beauty. They haven't ruined everything. The dolphins are here."

I smiled, the reminder of the reason for our trip erasing the tinge of homesickness.

"We're going to meet Calusa," he said, his excitement building again."She's the new baby in the pod. Born just a few months ago."

Perhaps it was the fact that the infant dolphin and Gabriel's daughter shared the name. Perhaps it was just the mention of a baby that triggered the pinch of self-loathing, but I heard the discomfort in my strained reply.

"Babies are wonderful. So are children. Really wonderful … I imagine."

"Yes," he said and laughed a little in that reflective way fathers do when their children are grown.

We moved over sparkling spans of aqua and passed between shadowy tunnels of chartreuse, lime, and jade and he recounted tales of raising his children. He spoke of the blue jays, pelicans, and squirrels that Calusa had rescued and nursed to health. He remembered his oldest son Ihasha's first swimming lessons in the Gulf of Mexico. He described the artistic talent, even as a boy, Carises had demonstrated in his cartoon drawings. Nodding and smiling, I tried, to the best of my ability, to appreciate and relate to his reminiscences, but somewhere inside of me I became acutely aware of an old wound festering open once again. It was a sting that had become duller as the sound of my biological clock's tick softened with each year's passing. But it had not yet ceased all together and it flared up unexpectedly to remind me of the unfulfilled aspect of my purpose as a woman.

"The kids love you," he said. I turned away from the unexpected sentiment, and pretended to watch all the unseen scenery flow by my window.

We did have an undeniable bond forming between us, but sometimes it seemed very fragile, without clear definitions of who we were to one another or who we might become over time. The woman who had given birth to them died while they were still adolescents and, by the close of my own adolescence, I had been warned that I should never attempt childbirth. It seemed at first glance as if our situations were suited for each other, but there existed a duality in the dynamics that both pulled us together and pushed us apart. With the grief that screamed in everything Gabriel's children did not speak about, with the echoing void that occupied the center of my femininity, and with the narrow age margin that separated Ihasha, Calusa, and Carises, from myself, we stepped willingly, yet cautiously, around each other.

On the edge of Marathon Key, just before the Seven Mile Bridge, Gabriel stopped at an open-air cafe. As I relaxed in the soothing heat of the noonday sun, the old ache dulled. In high spirits, Gabriel insisted on feeding me bites of his pie until he missed my mouth, and found my nose instead. His hand shook with laughter and he tipped the fork, depositing the bite of key lime onto my lap. I smirked, shook my head, and wiped pie from the tip of my nose, scooping the fallen filling off of my leg. There was a wonderful boy that lived inside the man, a boy who cried out for attention, for nurturing, for the mother he had never known.

As I reached across the table to take his hand, to reassure him, all the children denied mothers and all the mothers denied children suddenly converged in my conscience and the opening notes of a song that would forever carry with it the memories of my own mother's loss began to softly play somewhere deep inside my head.

***

She had been sitting on the floor, cross-legged, staring at the words and images that flowed across the screen. The disembodied voice of John Lennon sang of a world without hunger, greed, or reasons for killing as crowds huddled in the December twilight outside the Dakota. Some tossed piles of roses onto the dirty New York pavement. Others clutched Beatles albums to their chests. Men shook their heads and women covered their faces with gloved hands. Mom turned from the television and I saw the tears trailing her cheekbones.

"Someone shot him," she said quietly.

The screen flashed a photograph: Yoko smiling, John embracing her. "He's dead."

I knelt beside her and watched her cry as she watched the rest of the world weep; a London woman's trailing tears ran into the wet lines of grief framing an Asian face and became the tears of women in Toronto, in Johannesburg, in Rio de Janeiro, flowing towards one great river of shared sorrow.

When the news commentator segued clumsily from John and Yoko singing at a peace rally into the Reagan administration's latest Soviet policy, Mom frowned and turned off the volume.

"I am scheduled for surgery next week," she said, suddenly and unexpectedly changing topics.

With a confusing but very real sense of deep sadness cast by the assassination still clenching my stomach, I felt a buzz in my brain like a swarm of panic-stricken bees had been released. Why did she need surgery? My mother was the strong one in our family, the healthy one. She doctored the wounds on my father's feet that would not heal and had squeezed my hand before the surgeon wheeled the gurney into the operating room for my appendectomy. There was an unspoken understanding that seemed to exist in our family: my father and I were the patients, she was the care giver. If she had told me Dad or I was scheduled for a procedure or that one of us was to visit the hospital for a blood panel, I would not have experienced the churning in my gut that caused me to stammer when I finally found my voice.

"Are you sick? What's wrong? Why?"

She shook her head."No, I'm not sick. It's nothing like that, so please don't worry."

She pushed herself up from the floor and took a seat on the edge of the worn cushion of my father's favorite chair. The setting sunlight filtered between the blinds, throwing bars of shadow across her face and she wiped her eyes.

"Your dad," she started, hesitated, then began again, "your dad and I … we have decided that having more children would not be …" Her brow furrowed as she shuffled through mental lists of words for the most appropriate ones, the most neutral ones, the ones that, when said, would hurt the least."It wouldn't be a wise choice. Do you understand?"

A young girl should not have had to understand, but I did. On several nights, I had crouched in the doorway after they thought I was asleep, and listened to my parents' hushed battle drift down the hall from the kitchen."Diabetes" surfaced over and over in their dialogue, until it all made sense and I crawled back into bed and curled like a fetus. There, I rocked inside the safety of a quilted womb and sleep delivered nightmares of the monster wearing a mask that depicted my own horrified face as he tore wailing babies from my mother's arms.

"I understand," I said, the strange hollowness of my voice reflecting the kind of detachment other girls my age had not yet learned as a means of protection.

Years later, shortly before I turned eighteen, I would sit on the edge of an examination table as a specialist explained the possible negative effects of my brittle diabetes on an unborn child, high risk pregnancy, and his opinion on what would be my "wisest choice" and, again, in the same hollow voice I would acknowledge my understanding of a fate that seemed impossible to accept. With that, my father's apprehension and sense of responsibility and my mother's disappointment and lack of fulfillment had culminated, becoming the new burdensome bundle of mixed emotions that belonged to me, their daughter.

The nightly news had ended with another scene of the mourners outside the Dakota. The camera zoomed in on a woman cradling a faded Beatles album.

"I had that record when I was young," my mother suddenly said, as she glanced at the TV.

"Do you still have it?" I asked.

"No."

"What happened to it?"

"I brought it to a school dance," she said, "and someone stole it."

She got up from my father's chair then and went back to sit on the floor.

"Mom."

She turned, but did not say anything. She was crying again and in her eyes I saw the disappointment of a fifteen year old girl, walking home from the dance empty handed; I saw a tormented young mother cradling her chronically ill child; and I saw something I could not name, slowly draining away, until all that remained was the sterile white glint of the television in her pupils.

"I'm sorry."

The condolence could not lift the weight of personal responsibility I felt for her losses. I did not have the power to fix what had been broken nor retrieve what had been stolen. All I could do was curse the monsters in our midst: the invisible one that lived inside my father, thieving vitality from my mother; the inherited one that occupied me, robbing my family of happiness; and the insane ones that cowered behind guns, stealing peace from the world.

***

The rescued animals brought to the Dolphin Research Center on the shores of Grassy Key, had found a peaceful home there. It was a peace that extended to the people who staffed the facility, as well as to the visitors who came from all over the world to interact with their finned and feathered and furred relatives. Unlike most of the other all-too-numerous variety of marine attractions, there were no tanks or trainers or hoops to jump through at DRC. There were no loud speakers blaring upbeat techno music or bleachers filled with audiences screaming and clapping at imprisoned orcas and bottle nose. No one was forced to perform tricks for life forms with less compassion and intelligence than themselves.

Many of the dolphins who now lived in the protected lagoons of the center had once known such an existence, but still chose to fraternize with humans despite their histories. They understood that there were those who sought their purity of spirit and respected them as teachers, receptive to the wisdom they possessed.

In the reestablishment of their dolphin identities, a new kind of pod formed and mates found one another, their offspring, through blood lines, further strengthening the bond fate had initiated. Marina and Calusa were one of these mother-daughter pairs and, as I slipped on a wet suit and Gabriel took my cane to lead me to the dock's edge, the chilly water and exhilarating anticipation gripping every pore, they swam towards us and offered my first dolphin lesson.

Marina approached while Calusa darted around the lagoon's perimeter and observed her mother's interaction. With great patience and gentleness, Marina passed by where I floated and shivered, cold and excited, getting closer each time, until at last my hand made contact with her dorsal fin. In that moment, I was transformed, hearing joyous and spontaneous laughter bursting from my mouth, as unfamiliar and as mysteriously wonderful as the silky wet feel of her beautiful skin against my fingertips. Salty spray misted my face and blended with happy tears. We flew through the waves, a blissful sensation of weightlessness lifting me. I was that daring, free child I had always wished I could be. There were no monsters here. There wasn't any darkness, no unfillable emptiness. Just living flowing silver silk carrying me into the brilliant blue fusion of sea and sky.

From a distance, I could hear Gabriel's laughter echoing behind us like a skipped stone. Marina slowed, then stopped, and Calusa flashed passed, shrieking gleefully. I released her dorsal, preparing to tread water, not sure of my exact location in the lagoon, but, as I kicked my feet, my toes scraped something rough. A bit alarmed, I drew my knees towards my chest, keeping myself afloat with the motion of my arms. After a moment, I relaxed, and smiled, struck with the understanding of what Marina had done. Letting my feet drop, I stepped onto the mixture of shells, rocks and coarse sand. She had been aware of the fact that I could not see the dock and, if left in deeper water, would not have known which direction to swim. Marina had chosen to bring me to the shallows, where I could rest until she could give Gabriel a ride to the dock.

When he was safely grasping the end of the floating platform, Marina returned. As I heard her approach, I cupped my hand and again touched the most incredible flesh I had ever known. The strokes of her powerful tail could fracture a man's leg, and yet my guide propelled me with the tenderness of a mother into whose care a fragile infant has been entrusted. Nearing the platform, she left me an arm's length away from Gabriel, who reached out and grasped my hand, pulling me in.

"Look at you," he beamed, kissing my cheek."You're like a girl!"

It was true. But I was not the girl I had been in childhood. I was not the same child that hid under the hospital bed or the one who didn't receive slumber party invitations. I was no longer the little girl whose disease the kids on the playground all thought they could catch if they dared to jump rope with her. No, in that moment, my arms thrown around Gabriel's neck, with a smile so big my cheeks ached, I was someone new. I was the girl-child who flew through the ocean on the satin silver dorsal of a mother dolphin.

Returning from our swim, we stopped along the jetty, and rung the salt water from our hair. Gabriel recognized the larger shape of another dolphin moving languidly through the water at the far end of the lagoon. She kept her distance from the dock where several young females approached, whistling their shrill greetings.

"Do you remember Josephine?" the woman who acted as our facilitator asked when she noticed Gabriel watching the arch of the gray fin as it again breeched the surface in the distance.

He nodded, his response reflecting the same sincerity I had heard on his introduction to my grandmother. "I could never forget such an incredible lady."

"She's our resident queen. Loves to hold court with the young females. Enjoys their company, especially Theresa, the one that's expecting. But Jo doesn't interact very often any more with humans other than our staff members. I suppose that after all those years separated from her own kind, she just wants to make up for lost time. Had enough of people and their strange ways."

Gabriel winked at Theresa and her flirtatious friends. They rose on their tails, splashing and squealing at his attention, which caused the facilitator to grin.

"I think the girls are falling in love."

Across the lagoon, I heard the faint splash as Josephine dove then emerged again, and I felt my attention gently being tugged from the playful antics of Gabriel's latest fans. I turned slightly, touched the jetty's edge with the end of my cane, and listened for the sound of her almost imperceptible movements. As if she knew I was observing her with my ears, she slapped her broad tail once on the water's surface. The subtlety of it did not attract Gabriel's or the facilitator's notice. On a deeper level, a primal level, I believed that the communication was directed at me and I gave her my complete concentration.

She swam into my thoughts and tapped my intuitive and instinctual ancient center, tugging the cord that opens the mind to all the infinite possibilities. More crisp and clear then a photograph, more vivid than vision, she glided passed my mental eye: the beads of water rolling off her massive body: the powerful but graceful flick of her crescent tail; sunlight suspended in the mist of her outward breath; intellectand wisdom pooling in her liquid black eyes. Along with the feelings and the images came the question, nudging me forward, coaxing to be asked, although it did not seem to have been born of my own curiosity.

"Does Josephine have children?"

The facilitator paused, looking from the pregnant dolphin that frolicked near the jetty to her regal counterpart that slowly moved through the deeper water beyond. "No, she never gave birth. She was taken from her pod before she reached maturity and used for naval research for most of her adult life. When she arrived here, her reproductive years were already over."

Like a great tired sigh, Josephine released a long breath and disappeared below the rippling surface. At the base of the jetty, Theresa had lifted her head above the platform and spit streams of water up at Gabriel. The facilitator rolled her eyes.

"Okay, okay, Theresa. I'll bring him down to meet you."

We descended the steep wooden stairs to the dock and knelt at the edge. Theresa rolled onto her back, proudly sharing her swollen belly. We congratulated her on the upcoming event and doted on her beauty, which produced a lovely smile fully of tiny white teeth and more happy whistles and chattering.

"She likes it if you rub her tummy," the facilitator suggested.

All of the dolphins had been accommodating and had been very willing to "show" themselves to me. Even baby Calusa had, to the nervous gasps of the facilitator, displayed her tiny teeth by gingerly taking my hand in her mouth. Visitors were warned that it is better to avoid touching dolphins near the mouth, due to the many rows of needle-sharp teeth, but Calusa had decided, as the staff explained, that I deserved the full experience. After her teaching moment, she swam at lightning speed across the lagoon to her mother, obviously eager to tell Marina that she, too, had let the blind lady "see" her pearly whites.

The bond of love and acceptance I discovered in their presence brought clearer understanding of what Gabriel had meant when he had told me that he was bringing me to meet his dolphin family. Many of them had acknowledged the stone pendant that hung from a leather string around his neck, the only object he never took off.

"They're looking at our dolphins," he had whispered, noticing their observant gazes locating the silver companion that lay against my own throat.

They seemed to find pleasure in the articles, that, like feathers, quills, or paint worn by those who still considered themselves traditional native people, were worn with a sense of honor, respect, and spiritual significance. The pendants were more than jewelry, more than decoration. They were medicine, and the dolphins knew that Gabriel and I saw them as such.

Theresa's show of trust further exemplified the mysterious resonance that I experienced, more tightly weaving their pure energy with the energy of my own spirit and, as I extended my palm above her pregnant belly, I felt as if I were about to cradle *Wakan Tanka*, the Great Holy Mystery, in my hand. But the mixture of emotions that welled up when my fingers caressed the round fullness and I imagined the beautiful unborn being beneath it proved the duality of everything that exists within the Mystery. It was the same tug of war between the lightness of happiness and the unbearable burden of desolation I had known once when my dear sister-friend, Rita, had unexpectedly placed my hand on her stomach and I felt Julia pressing her tiny elbow or knee or foot towards the world outside. My heart had swelled while my womb closed in upon itself, becoming another dry bitter raisin, and resentment pounded in my head, its echo ringing through my emptiness.

But Gabriel's voice silenced the echo."Josephine," he said.

As the facilitator rose to her feet, stunned by what she saw, the old dolphin swam slowly towards the platform. Theresa rolled and moved aside, along with her young companions, as they made room for their matriarch. Much larger than the others, Josephine labored to maneuver her massive body closer to the dock, adjusting her position several times until her head was within my reach.

"We're honored, Grandmother," Gabriel said.

She raised her head and stroked her mandrel against my fingers. Turning her face, she directed my hand towards her eye, then her blow hole, exposing sensitive areas that usually were off limits to human touch. She rolled and turned, granting me permission, granting me her trust. Tenderly, I rubbed her satin skin, as its fragile beauty unfolded like a forgotten gown retrieved from the depths of an antique steamer trunk, the texture muted with the invisible dusty thin layers of time that spoke only to the touch of its ancient age.

"This is really unusual," the facilitator said, slightly baffled."Jo hasn't interacted with visitors in quite a while."

The younger females, out of reverence to the elder, stayed a short distance from the platform and did not vie for the attention as they had with each other. Theresa, especially attentive to Josephine's out-of-the-ordinary human contact, watched intently.

My hand slid over the great silver gray body, our physical connection never breaking, our mental connection growing, until my fingers neared the jagged scar along her flank. Before I reached it, she pulled back, not allowing me to see the mark of her past, not allowing me any opportunity to feel the pity contact with the old wound would have created. That was not the message she brought. It was not the teaching she wished to leave in her wake.

She pivoted, water lapping over the platform onto my knees as her head stopped less than a foot from mine, my mind's eye meeting the bottomless black pools of wisdom staring back at me.

And the voice came, strong and clear, as it traveled from some external source, although it seemed to exist only to the ear within as sound.

It might have been confused as one of my own thoughts, had it not been so clear, so distinct, so separate.

The name "mother" is not earned through the endeavors of the womb; it is earned through the endeavors of the heart.

Then Josephine sank back away from where I knelt. I whispered my gratitude, as she returned to the far side of the lagoon.

CHAPTER TWENTY-ONE

WINTER OF
THE HOWLING WOLF

The howling persisted from behind the locked door and the island dogs barked wildly, as their not-so-distant lupine DNA responding to her primal plea. Strangers were in the den, humans she did not recognize. The great mane of black and tan hair rose from her neck and she threw her head back, nostrils flaring, and unleashed another mournful cry that vibrated the window glass throughout the house. In the deepest darkness of the pre-dawn hour, I hung on the rim of consciousness, teetering on the brink of shock, and hovered ever closer to the edge of death. Only the wolf's howl still connected my mind to consciousness and I clung to it, one clear thought rising above the murky confusion. I needed to go to her. I had to confront whatever, whoever had caused her distress. I must rescue Istazi.

"We adopted her from Federal Wolf Dog Rescue."

Istazi had pressed her head to my waist, fixing the intense yellow eyes for which she had been named on the inquisitive interloper, as Gabriel had addressed another round of the frequently asked questions the three of us always seemed to attract.

"Is it full blooded wolf?" the driver of the Escalade said, leaning a bit further out the window to gawk.

Gabriel's forearm tensed beneath my hand and Istazi moved in order to position herself between me and the driver, staring so intently that the man was the first to look away. I hated the question, too. It ranked right up there with "Are you part Indian?" and "Are you totally blind?" But Gabriel and I sat on the rescue organization's board of directors and, despite our personal annoyance, we tried to practice diplomacy.

"She is gray wolf and Malamute," I said, again emphasizing that Istazi was a "she" and not to be confused with the pronoun used to describe a shoe or a lamp or a box of snack crackers.

"How much wolf?"

I bit the inside of my lip. Wolves and Indians. Indians and wolves. How inseparable our lives, how similar our histories. Since the European invasion and occupation began at Plymouth, we had been feared, hunted, and slaughtered, our stories often cross-referenced. Dee Brown's *Bury My Heart at Wounded Knee* recounted a chilling statement of a nineteenth century United States Army officer. As his troops massacred over a hundred Arapaho men, women, and children and burned their village to the ground, it was recorded that he shouted, "We must kill them all. We must kill them like wolves."

Brown's book revealed another grim historical incident. Venturing outside the boundaries of the reservation, a group of starving Nakota people who had been cheated out of the government rations promised them by treaty found piles of meat. Ravaged by malnutrition and desperate to save the lives of their children and elders, they took the meat, too hungry to question its source. When the Nakota who ate the food began to die agonizing deaths, it was discovered that the venison had been laced with arsenic and placed as bait. The rancher who had planted the deadly meal had intended it for wolves; he offered no apology nor faced any criminal charges for the deaths of the Nakota.

No matter whether it was directed at Istazi or Gabriel or me, "how much" seemed to carry with it deeper unspoken meanings. Why was the question of "how much" so important to so many? Did it determine how much we should be hated, how much we should be trusted, how much we should be accepted? Did the answer establish how much we should be feared?

"Florida law allows for animals three quarters wolf and less without a wildlife permit," I said, hoping the general fact would suffice as an answer.

Istazi nuzzled my hand and my fingers found the spot behind her ears where she liked to be scratched. We did not actually know her origins, but it had always been clear, through her behavior, that she knew who she was and with which aspect of her genetics she most identified herself. The trivial trappings of human labels did not define her existence. As if bored with his curiosity, she looked at the driver and yawned.

"Look at those teeth," he said."She must be really ferocious."

The comment produced a smile as I thought of the gentle way she laid her head on my lap when we sat on the couch together or how she preened Maakwa, the cat's, thick hair with her front teeth like a mother cleaning her pup. Of course, the capability to harm or even kill existed within her, a fact realized every time she took the raw chicken leg quarters we fed her from my hand and crunched the femur bone in half with a single bite. But the capability was not fueled by aggression, aggression being a trait which humans had bred into the lupine's nearest cousin, the domesticated dog.

Wolves, when faced with fight or flight, always chose the latter and, although the myth of the vicious wolf fairytales had provoked early European settlers to hunt them to near extinction, not one account of wolves killing a human had ever been recorded in American history.

Unfortunately, facts lagged behind fiction for most people and the *Little Red Riding Hood* and *Three Little Pigs* versions still prevailed along-side Hollywood's depiction of Indians as whooping, scalping savages, and sports fans in the nation's capital cheered a football team called the "Redskins".

"Wolves are very protective of their own," I said."I wouldn't want to be the person she assessed might be a threat to one of us. Our family pack has a strong bond. It's all about respect."

"Well, she's extremely beautiful," the driver said, looking up from Istazi to eye Gabriel and me."By the way, are the two of you Native American?"

Istazi tugged on the leash, urging us off the road and towards the park. Gabriel cleared his throat."We have to keep moving," he said."She needs her exercise."

Apparently miffed that we no longer showed interest in being a living roadside exhibit, the SUV's dark tinted window slid shut and roared off. He had never offered his name. He hadn't offered a thank you. He hadn't even offered so much as a good-bye.

When we reached the park's interior, we stopped under a cluster of palms and squatted in the shade next to Istazi. Gabriel stroked her fluffy coat and said, "Thanks for the assist."

She licked his face and her bushy tail swayed from side to side. Turning, she had covered my face with kisses, too.

"Nice save, my girl. Very nice save"

***

"You saved me. I could have...," I stammered, my body still shaking under the sweat-soaked night shirt.

Gabriel wrapped his arms tighter around me, trying to stop my shivers, trying to stop his tears.

"Shh," he whispered, not letting me finish."I know. I know."

Istazi sniffed anxiously at the bandage on my hand where the paramedics had administered the intravenous glucose. Then she jumped onto the bed to smell my breath and to lick the perspiration from my face. When she had completed her thorough examination, she curled all hundred and ten pounds into a compact circle at my feet and watched the door for the strangers whose antiseptic scent still lingered in the bedroom. Burying my fingers in her silky coat, I clung to her with one hand and to Gabriel's arm with the other, feeling more afraid, more fragile, but more grateful than I had ever felt.

"What do you remember?" he asked.

"Istazi was howling. She sounded so far away."

"Is that the first thing you were aware of?"

"Yes. And then I tried to wake up because I wanted to console her. All those dogs were barking and I sensed somebody in the room. Then I felt them injecting something in my hand and I thought for a moment that I was being abducted. Thought aliens were performing some kind of experiment."

"Not star beings, honey. EMT."

I nodded as I remembered how their voices had reached into the haze, loudly urged me to tell them my name, my age, and asked me if I knew who Gabriel was, if I could identify my location.

"I couldn't wake you. When I heard you moaning, I touched you. You were drenched in sweat, so I started shaking you but you didn't respond. Then I sat you up and ran to get orange juice. But you'd fallen over before I could get back and I fought to pull you upright again. You wouldn't drink it and you slumped over again, knocked the glass out of my hand, and clenched your teeth. That's when I called 911."

I listened, with no recollection of the events he described.

"When the ambulance arrived, I took Istazi and Maakwa into the office and shut the door. I wasn't sure if they would allow strangers near you in the bedroom. I was frantic and they were, too. When the paramedics came in and started working on you, she started howling."

I broke then, sobbing against his chest, as the magnitude of what had happened crushed me with guilt. I had been asleep, oblivious to the signs of my dangerously low blood sugar level; something, in thirty years, I had never done. Diabetes had almost won this time. It had almost snatched me away in the middle of the night as it had fatally accomplished with other victims. The monster had almost killed me.

As dawn crept closer, we laid awake in the stillness. I was exhausted from the ordeal, but fought to keep my eyes open, apprehensive of what sleep might bring, until Gabriel told me to let go, that he would watch over me. Istazi remained curled at our feet and Maakwa sprawled on the pillow above my head. His tail brushed slowly against my neck and soothed me towards slumber. Although the coming day would bring a cool dry wind from the north and transition into what we called "wolfie weather," Istazi would decline Gabriel's invitation to play chase in the back yard. She and Maakwa would refuse to leave my side until, still feeling the rawness of having been emotionally and physically turned inside out, I would drag myself from bed.

I pulled on a robe, my body laboring under what could best be described as a diabetic hangover, as Istazi lifted her head to scrutinize my every move. Hearing her loud, rapid pants, an audible cue she always used to gain my attention, I assured her that I would only be across the hall and that I would be all right. She sprang off the bed anyway. When I came out of the bathroom, she sat in the hallway, waiting just outside the door. She buried her head in the folds of my robe and I knelt to embrace her. Melting into one another, my tears fell and clung in her dense coat.

"You are truly a sacred being."

With a meow too big for a house cat, Maakwa sauntered up and rubbed against Istazi's legs, then mine. I scooped him up and kissed his nose.

"Yes, you're sacred, too."

He purred, satisfied, and licked a tear from my chin. Although he was the smallest member of our pack, he never let anyone overlook him.

Gabriel sat in the hammock, gazing up into the canopy of the java plum tree. A pair of cardinals, one male, one female, darted from branch to branch, their high sweet voices calling to one another as they flew. Istazi and I stepped out onto the patio.

"My girls," he greeted, as I took a cane from beside the back door and walked down the path he had created especially for me that lead to the hammock.

Flashing him an adorable toothy smile, Istazi trotted off to the side yard to dig in the sand. I dropped the cane next to the path and he pulled me onto his lap.

"I checked on you every ten minutes. I promise."

"Oh, no, it's okay! You shouldn't be stuck in the house watching me sleep on such a beautiful afternoon. That wouldn't be fair."

We rocked in the breeze and listened to the cardinals singing and to the squirrels chasing each other around the trunk of the oak tree. I rested my head on his shoulder and smelled the scent of sage and sweet grass.

"I cleansed the house with smoke and the rattle," he said. "I prayed with the pipe." His voice cracked. "I almost lost you."

He didn't deserve the terror that I had put him through. It didn't matter that it wasn't intentional; I was still the source.

I remembered the alarm and the subsequent antipathy I had felt as a teenager when, after my parents had separated, I returned home long past my mother's appointed curfew. But she had no longer been there to enforce it and my father had no longer seemed to care. As I moved in the dark, trying to avoid the hall's squeaky floor boards, I had heard him calling for me. I asked, "What is it, Dad?" But he just kept saying my name.

When I had switched on the light, I found everything Gabriel had described: a drenched T-shirt, clenched teeth, shaking, moaning. I had run to the kitchen, dumped more table sugar into the orange juice, and ran back to the bed, pouring it into his mouth. He had jerked his head from side to side, which spilled the sticky juice on the blanket. My father's eyes had been like the glassy eyes of a fish staring up through the waves at a waterless world above that he could not fathom. When he continued not to cooperate and pressed his lips shut, I, no longer knowing what to do, had yelled at him.

"Drink the fucking juice or I'm calling the ambulance!"

Perhaps my frantic screaming, like Istazi's howl, became the lifeline he had needed, because he loosened his lips and let the orange juice be poured into his mouth until his eyes lost their unnatural shininess and he took the glass for himself. At eighteen, I had yet to experience all of the cruel possibilities of diabetes firsthand and could not understand how my father had let his blood sugar drop that low without taking action. Hostility forced me to find somewhere to place the blame and I divided it in half. I pointed a finger at him for his irresponsibility and pointed another finger at my mother for having abandoned her caregiver's post.

Now, as I listened to the ripe fruit falling from the plum tree and landing hard against the purple-stained earth, my heart ached with the knowledge of how unfair I had been for having blamed anyone.

"Gabe," I said and touched his face, "are you sure about all this? I would understand if you weren't. Are you certain you can love someone like me, someone who's so broken?"

He took my hand from his cheek and kissed my palm and my fingertips. I closed my eyes and an inner voice urged for him to take the opportunity and run, escape, while yet another begged for him to never leave.

"You aren't broken."

His lips pressed to one eyelid, then the other. I became self-conscious of my hard plastic prostheses beneath them and pulled back, but he embraced me closer and kissed them some more.

"You are not broken, my love. You're not broken," he whispered. "You're beautiful and whole and I love you for everything you are. Everything."

The founder of the rescue organization, who had lived among wolves and wolf dogs for many years, had once spoken of the loyalty of certain animals. She said, "Some have unbearable lives before they're rescued. When adopted, they possess a greater appreciation of good homes and loving families. Rescues know they have been given a second chance. They don't forget it."

Maakwa peered out the back window at Istazi as she came around the side of the house. Pausing, she looked at him, standing on the sill, and their noses touched through the screen. Climbing from the hammock, Gabriel lifted my white cane from among the fallen plums and took my hand, helping me up. Our fingers interlocked in the natural easy way they always did as we moved through life together and we walked, hand-in-hand, up the path. Gabriel carried the cane.

We all were the rescued. We all were the rescuers. In this pack, none would ever forget it.

PART III

SUMMER SOLSTICE

2006

We raised the sacred pipe to the morning sky, offering it to the east as the sun's first rays tinted the crowns of the palms golden, ushering in the beginning of a new season, the season of growth, of warmth, of light. Where tide had touched earth, the white sand was still cool and damp against our bare feet as we stood in the ceremonial circle.

Transcending the lingering layers of mist, thin fingers of purifying smoke rose from an abalone shell at the circle's center as the cedar and sage smoldered. I felt Gabriel's hand beside mine as we grasped the pipe stem and the four eagle feathers that adorn it stirred in the motionless air, sweeping lightly across our arms like the outward breath of something too powerful and mysterious to exist within the boundaries of explanation.

We addressed Wakan Tanka, the Great Mystery, with an expression of gratitude to the universe and everything that subsists within it and an acknowledgement of our sacred connection to it all. The ocean lapped softly onto the shore and our voices rose and fell with the wave's gentle rhythm.

Then Gabriel moved his hands along the pipe until one covered my fingers wrapped around the stem and the other cupped the hand cradling the bowl.

"Thank you for your love," he said. "Thank you for sharing this life with me. Thank you for walking this path as my companion."

The moon had not yet set even as the sun broke over the trees suspending the moment amid the two celestial bodies like a pendulum poised at the seam between darkness and light, night and day, past and future. I rested my eyes on his face, and smiled at his image, seeing it so clearly in my mind.

"Thank you for your love. Thank you for showing me beauty. Thank you for your light."

He lit a match then, touching the flame to the bowl, and we put the stem to our mouths, drawing in and sending out our prayers on the sweet tobacco smoke. How many generations, infused with European blood and religious indoctrination, had come into this world and passed into the next without knowledge of this ceremony? How many summers had come and gone since one of my ancestors last celebrated the solstice? Who had been the last relative to offered prayers without bowed head and clasped hands? Had the old woman who appeared to me when I was still a little girl been the one?

Whomever it had been, however long ago, however far the distance separating our shared spiritual experience, time's gap closed as I held the pipe and smoked. All that had been forgotten was remembered. Everything that had once been denied was acknowledged. The hidden primal spark living in my blood burned bright and strong as a circle, once broken, became whole once more.

We smoked until the round red bowl was empty and the last ribbons of smoke vanished with the dawn, the sun spreading its rays over the dunes and across the white sand to the ocean, casting myriad sparkling lights on the water's surface. I took Gabriel's arm and we stepped from the circle and walked into the slow roll of the surf. As the waves broke around our knees, a light wind blew out of the north and brushed my cheek. It brought thoughts of my father.

Once, a few years before, he and I had walked together on this same stretch of sand. Colors filled the sky above the Gulf of Mexico as the setting sun shone behind the mountain clouds all red and orange and yellow. As night waited at our backs, my father had taken my hand and, although his continuing battle with diabetes had left him thin and a little frail, I felt great power in his grip. Despite his many life-threatening bouts with the monster, his chapped knuckles and palms were reminders of the decades he had labored with car parts and factory machinery. It would take almost fifty years of chronic illness, an amputation, a heart attack, kidney and pancreas transplants, and two strokes to force his retirement. Less than a year shy of his sixty-fifth birthday, he finally laid down his tools. Gabriel said that my father was a warrior, the kind of man other men could respect, the kind of father a daughter should honor.

Looking out across the breaking waves at the ending day before turning his gaze towards my face, my father had spoken."It's beautiful here," he said."Do you like living by the ocean? Are you happy?"

I nodded."I'm very happy here. It's peaceful."

Pleased, he pressed my fingers with his then continued."Is Gabe looking after you? Is he good to you?"

"Yes, he's wonderful to me. He loves me."

"He's a good man," my father said, his voice faltering with emotions he rarely showed.

Hugging me, he expressed his love. I said that I loved him, too. And then we both were weeping, suddenly shaken by the recollection of life's changes, so strongly aware that there would always be more on the horizon.

"It's been tough, hasn't it?" he said.

We shared the battle strain of our war with the monster and the way it had sometimes drawn us closer, but, more often, had caused us to keep each other at arm's length. But as we held on to one another in those last moments of twilight, everything that we had never said, could never address, became the acknowledgement wrapped up in that one question.

"Yes," I said."But it's easier now, isn't it?"

He exhaled, long and slow, as if he had taken the breath years ago and had been waiting to release it ever since my birth.

"I'm proud of you, Amy."

Gently releasing from his embrace, I had taken my father's hand and let go of my own long-held breath.

***

The solstice sun shone on the pelicans' wings as they glided on the warm currents and Gabriel inhaled the salty morning air, the new day waiting at our backs. I ran my hand along the braid of hair resting between his shoulder blades.

"Do you remember when we were first together and you wondered what it was that I saw? You wondered whether there is nothing else, only darkness."

Perhaps few sighted people considered what existed when a blind woman opens her eyes because no one before Gabriel had ever asked. But, from the very beginning of our relationship, he had wanted to understand and relate to my blind life; a desire that touched me and sometimes made me laugh. I had once caught him, eyes closed, lights off, hunting for the can opener in the kitchen drawer. He thought his maiden voyage into sightless waters had been a success, until we both realized he was trying to get baked beans out of the can with a garlic press. I had appreciated his effort and had congratulated him for not slicing his fingers on the knives we stored in the same drawer. He deserved to know what I saw, but was surprised by the actual answer.

At first, I experienced what most would imagine those with total blindness to possess: a dark murky color, very dull and flat, one shade shy of true black. But as I gradually healed, emotionally as well as physically, the view shifted and something strange and unexpected grew out of the gloom.

"My point of light is very bright right now. The colors are there, too," I said, smiling up at him.

Like a milk-white moon suspended in an inner cosmos, the solid circle of light floated, expanding and brightening with my positive emotions, joy, love, peace, laughter, passion, and creativity sending shooting star sparks to orbit around it. With harmony, colors often appeared, as for long moments the white light pulsed shades of blue, green, red, purple, or yellow. Concentration let me increase the size and brightness of the mysterious light, but the colors always came at their own accord; a gift beyond my control.

But whether my happiness tossed a million spiraling sparks from its edges or its shine dulled with my sadness, the light lived in my blind field of vision. It always changed, but never left.

His voice was soft and serious and beautiful as he said, "Ceremony attracts and releases great power. Our spirits respond to it."

The light swelled, flashing pink, turning to poppy, becoming red, then deepening to the crimson of my suffering and my salvation, my loss and my reward, my body's fragility and my spirit's endurance. It was the color of my disease and my destiny. It was the color of wholeness.

It was *oyate duta*, the red nations, the color of my people.

It was the color of blood.

EPILOGUE

2010

My father did not recognize me (at first),
My father did not recognize me (at first).
When again he saw me,
When again he saw me,
He said, "You are the offspring of a crow,"
He said, "You are the offspring of a crow."

-*Ghost Dance Song*, Titanka Iyanke (Sitting Bull)

Suddenly, in the distance, approaching from every direction, I heard the crows cawing, and then, all at once, their shadows flew across the earth around me; not a bird in sight. Cradled in my hand, the intersect where the pipestone meets the wood of the stem became my father's flesh, and, in that sacred moment, I retreated one year, and the memory, released from where I had caged it, flew free.

I was with my father on that morning, the morning after Thanksgiving, that bright, frigid South Dakota morning. I held him close, a hand beneath his neck, the other on his chest, and murmured into his ear, "I love you. It's all right. You're free now."

I felt his cold perspiration against my palms, the sound of the ragged rasp of his labored breaths imprinting upon my memory forever, until the last exhalation passed his lips, and my touch registered the final beat of my father's heart.

In the circularity of life itself, he had been there when I entered the world and took the first breath, and I with him upon his exit and his last. It was the good death of a warrior, and, in the traditional ways of our Lakota ancestors, in the manner befitting a warrior's daughter, I cut my hair. Now it lies with him, within the earth, within the embrace of our Mother.

The year following his death moved like winter through my bones, and the crows came often, bringing his name on wings the color of obsidian."Your grandfather gave me the name Merle," my father had once said."It means black bird."

So when the day that marked the end of my year of mourning arrived, I was not surprised that an enigmatic form of the familiar black birds attended our pipe ceremony. Their shadows were cast from a space neither of this world nor of the next, but one that exists between that which we consider tangible and that which we know as spiritual. Wise beyond human wisdom, the crows raised their disembodied voices until the reverberation echoed through the trees like an ancient chant, a chant that honored the memory of my father.

About the Author

Amy Krout-Horn worked as the first blind teaching assistant at the University of Minnesota's American Indian Studies program. She is a regular contributor to Slate and Style magazine and, in 2008, was awarded their top fiction prize for *War Pony*. She co-authored the novella, *Transcendence* (All Things That Matter Press, 2009). Her creative non-fiction was featured in the spring 2010 issue of Breath and Shadow, and Talking Stick Native Arts Quarterly published her essay, *Bleeding Black*, in their fall 2010 issue. Currently, she is at work on her third novel, *Dancing in Concrete Moccasins*.

A staunch advocate for social and environmental justice, she writes and lectures on native history and culture, diabetes and disability, and humanity's connection and commitment to the natural world. For more information, visit her web site at www.nativeearthwords.com

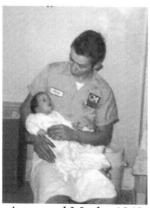

Amy and Merle, 1969

ALL THINGS THAT MATTER PRESS ™

FOR MORE INFORMATION ON TITLES AVAILABLE FROM
ALL THINGS THAT MATTER PRESS, GO TO
http://allthingsthatmatterpress.com
or contact us at
allthingsthatmatterpress@gmail.com

Made in the USA
Lexington, KY
22 May 2013